An Illustrated Explanation of Eco-Electricity

D. W. Cockburn

An Illustrated Explanation of Eco-Electricity

Contents

Overview

To provide the UK with entirely environmentally friendly and economical electricity; we need to make our electricity generating and distribution systems, as well as our electrical propulsion systems as 'green' and efficient as possible.

Making do and mending what we already have and providing innovative ideas for the future are therefore our 'goals.'

Electricity Generation:

With good reason, we are going to be using only 'green' electricity generating systems in the future and to be at their most efficient, all the alternative methods of generating this 'green' electricity should eventually be located within areas of the globe that are the most suitable and appropriate for their use.

Solar panels; which can turn light and heat into electrical power, will always be at their most efficient when located around the Earths' Equator where the sunlight/heat is abundant.

Wind turbines; which can turn the force of wind into electrical power, will always be at their most efficient when located within the Polar regions or at an extremely high altitude where the force of wind is abundant, and the ambient temperatures are 'low.' This is not only because of the comparatively large volume of electrical power that can be generated or the comparatively low 'resistance' to electrical power distribution but, located in these regions wind turbines will also avoid flying birds as much as possible.

Hydro-electric power generation; which captures and releases rainwater at a regulated flow rate, when used on inland waterways anywhere around the world will inevitably encourage Governments to keep those waterways clean, fast flowing, and free from obstructions.

Tidal-stream electrical power generation; which harnesses the motion of the tides of the sea, can be located all around the coastline of every land mass on the face of the planet, not only generating a plentiful regulated supply of 'green' electricity but also creating safe havens for fish to….. do whatever it is fish do.

Electricity Storage:

The storage (or the 'regulation' of the output) of electrical power when 'intermittently' generated by Solar panels and Wind turbines situated in inappropriate locations around the world; should always make the 'full' cost of their use prohibitive.

Electricity Distribution:

The big drawback that we currently have in the UK with regards to our 'National Grid' electrical power distribution system; is the fact that it is an 'air cooled' system!

Suspending electrical conductors from pylons high above the ground as the main part of a power distribution system not only means that the electrical conductors used must be able to carry their own weight over long distances, but it also leaves us unable to manually control the ambient temperature of the air surrounding those electrical conductors.

Therefore; to efficiently distribute the 'green' electrical power that we can now generate, our National Grid system really needs to be re-located underground. Because housed within temperature-controlled tunnels in the form of an unbroken loop all around the coast of the UK, it will be possible to effectively connect individual electrical power generating systems together to create a subterranean, temperature-controlled (therefore a 'variable/lowerable resistance'), electrical power distribution grid system.

Efficiency of Existing Electricity Distribution systems:

To ensure that there is no wastage of electrical power unnecessarily through our existing 'low voltage' (up to and including 500v ac) electrical systems; these 'low voltage' systems need inspecting and (critically) 'testing'. Then those test results need to be evaluated to find and to 'clear' these systems of any loose connections, badly warn switches or socket outlets, earth leakage problems, earth faults, and overcurrent protection issues, all of which waste power, create unwanted heat, and/or send electrical current straight back to the mass of the earth unused.

Electrical Propulsion systems:

Simply replacing the internal combustion powered crankshaft like for like, with multiple electric-motor powered crankshafts will offer sharper throttle response and better balance to any current motorised vehicle from a moped, via Hawker Hurricanes to a super-tanker.

The concept of turning electricity into Hydrogen and then turning that Hydrogen back into electricity to power an electric motor, will waste 40% of the electricity before that electric-motor is even energised; which seems illogical to me and therefore a bit of a non-starter.

The 'key' to the conundrum of the electric vehicle 'range' is the battery-bank 'on-board charging system,' which means that we require methods and battery-bank compositions that can generate and accept charging 'quickly' both when the vehicle is stationary and whilst the vehicle is in motion.

We have an awful lot to be grateful to the internal combustion engine for as well as steam power, wind power, waterpower and the 'beasts of burden' that they replaced, after all acceleration is the only human-caused sensation, but the bottom line is:

"Fossil fuels are great, but they stink"!

This book contains simplified illustrations, accompanied by written explanations of how we can achieve all the 'goals' above:

Efficient Electrical Power Generation

Climate change is a global problem and therefore if we are to supply all the people in the world including the UK with an inexhaustible supply of 'green' energy, efficient electrical power generation requires a global solution.

The UK is just an island in the North Sea, with a higher-than-average amount of rainfall, therefore 'water management' is the key to our independence regarding electrical power generating. The quantity of rainfall and the rugged nature of the terrain in Wales and Scotland make both Countries ideal locations to exploit inland waterways with the use of hydro-electric power generation, whilst the constant motion of the seas around our entire coastline can be exploited by using tidal-stream electrical power generation harnessing the motion of the tides.

Harnessing tidal-stream power around the UK:

To harness power generated by the motion of the tides in the 'horizontal' plane;

The use of 'just' sub-marine turbines located close to the shore all around the coast of the UK can ensure smooth power delivery over an entire 24-hour period, because the tide turns at contrasting times in separate locations. The location of submarine turbines must be co-ordinated carefully to ensure that there are no gaps in electricity generating at any time over any given 24-hour period; with the tides turning as they do at 'slack water' each turbine will stop four times a day therefore, if 'just' turbines are used we must allow for the fact that at any given time somewhere around the coastline at least one (or one group of) turbine(s) will always be stationary.

To harness power generated by the motion of the tides in the 'vertical' plane;

The use of 'just' buoyant, cantilever come pump/piston arrangements close to the shore all around the coast of the UK can also ensure smooth power delivery over an entire 24-hour period. A multiple cantilever system could work as an independent generating system using the same principle as when using submarine turbines in the horizontal plane, but the advantage of the cantilever system over the turbine system is the ease of 'storage' of the 'power output,' when power is generated in the vertical plane simply because we have 'gravity' working with us. The power output 'regulating' properties of a cantilever system can also be useful for mechanically storing electrical power within a single generating device which combines both a cantilever system and a turbine!

To harness power generated by the motion of the tides in the 'horizontal' and the 'vertical' plane simultaneously;

Humankind has now produced something that I like to describe as a "Spitfire on a stick" because that is what it looks like from the landward angle, but as all of them are to be located under water most people will never see one. Therefore;

A "Spitfire on a stick" is a 'seamless tidal-stream electricity generating system,' capable of generating 'regulated output' electricity 'independently,' 24 hours a day 7 days a week!

Therefore; it is not only the lower overall power output required over the shorter distances from 'submarine generators' (when compared to offshore wind turbines) needed to maintain potential difference (voltage) in our electrical power distribution system, nor is it only the predictable regularity of the gravitational pull of the Moon that gives tidal-stream generation the advantage over wind (and/or solar) power for the UK, but also; it is the fact that the 'motion' of the seas tides being in both the 'horizontal' and the 'vertical' plane 'simultaneously,' can be invaluable when 'regulating' the output of the electricity generated (which can otherwise be costly)!

<u>Harnessing power globally</u>:

Wind Turbines:

Wind turbines ideally need to be in areas of the world where birds do not fly to allow the turbines to rotate freely and at maximum speed, therefore allowing them to generate their maximum potential power output. Ideal locations in terms of efficiency for wind turbines would therefore be, for example; extremely high up in the Himalayan Mountain region, or at the South Pole, or in Alaska, Siberia, or northern Canada all of which also have exceptionally low ambient temperatures that make the distribution of the power generated within those regions comparatively inexpensive.

Wind turbines are presently an 'unregulated' source of generating electrical power, therefore the cost of the wind turbine itself is only a part of the overall cost of their use. The power that is generated needs to be stored in some way so that it can then be released at a constant flow rate when it is needed, and the storage capacity may need to be very large indeed when employed in inappropriate locations because of the unpredictable nature of wind, many days' worth of power will need to be mechanically stored to allow for the fact that the wind may not blow for days.

Solar Panels:

The ideal location for solar panels in terms of efficiency are in the desert regions around the Earths' equator as there is little or no rain making cleaning the panels easier, daylight hours are the longest both in hours per day and in days per year and the ambient temperature is high. All of which serve to allow us to harness the maximum amount of potential power from each solar cell.

As with wind turbines, solar panels are presently an 'unregulated' source of generating electrical power, therefore again, the cost of the solar panel is only a 'part' of the overall cost of their use. The power that they generate again, needs storing and the output regulating for release over the entire 24-hours of the day; and large batteries are not cheap!

Fossil fuels & Nuclear power:

We do not need to waste oil, gas, coal, or nuclear power energizing electricity distribution systems anywhere inside the circumference of the orbit of our Moon, because the gravitational pull of our Moon is the most powerful 'force' that we can harness in this part of this Solar System!

Rather than generating electricity using fossil fuels or nuclear power within the Earths' atmosphere, in the future nuclear power can be solely for jet engine 'turbine' propulsion which, when combined with 'combustible' bio or fossil fuels injected into a jet propulsion systems' compression chamber; can provide thrust for an extremely powerful jet propulsion system of considerable range for future use 'outside' of the Earths' atmosphere!

This is not the end of the fossil fuel, biofuel, or nuclear industries, this is just the beginning!

The Principle of Gravity Power Storage

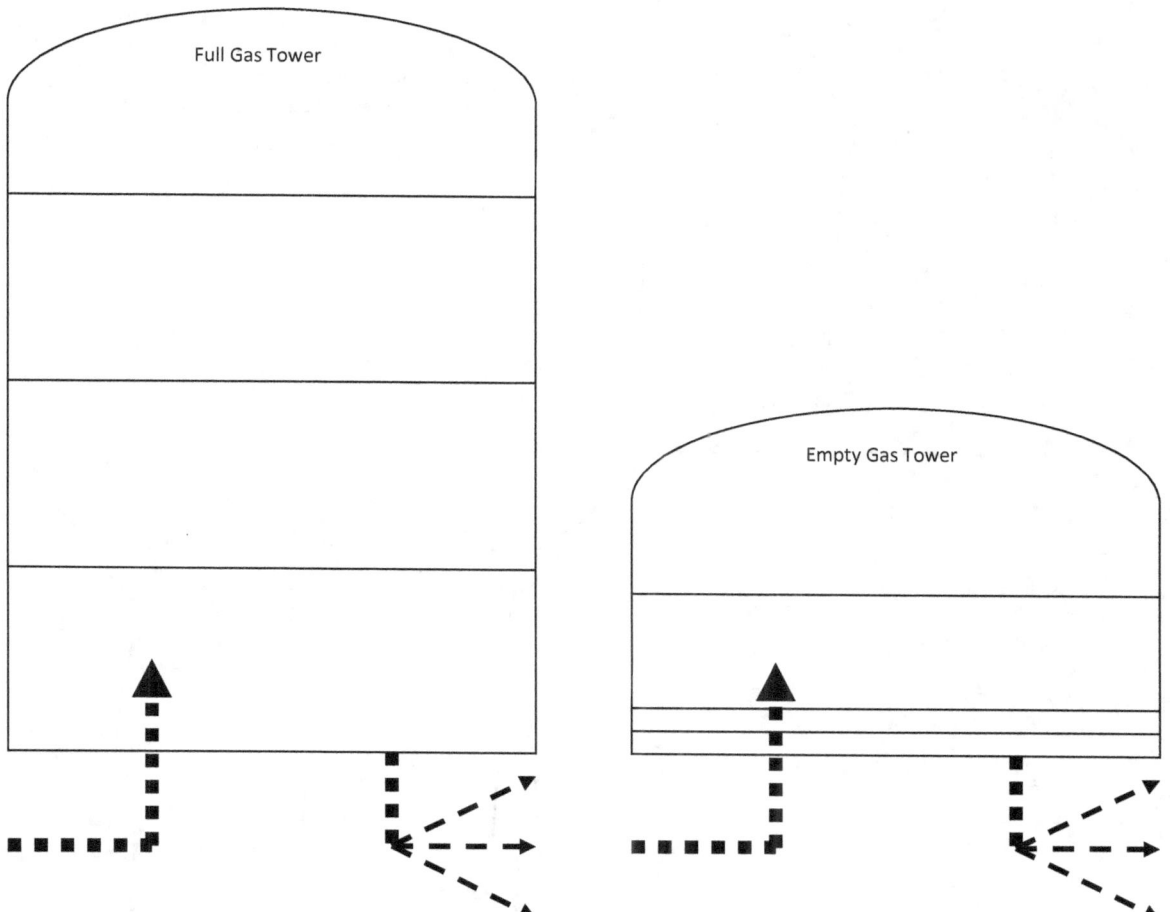

Above is a simplified representation of two 'Gas Towers,' one of which is full and the other empty. Gas is pumped in at very high pressure which lifts the heavy metal dome on the top of the tower to its' highest point, then as the gas is used up supplying gas central heating/hot water and cooking appliances the heavy metal dome comes down under the force of 'gravity' maintaining pressure in the supply of gas to those appliances as it falls.

A similar system could be used to store the electrical power generated by wind turbines or solar panels: whilst it is windy or sunny and they are generating electricity, the electricity generated can be used to lift the heavy metal dome which can then be released to fall under its' own weight and its' downward 'motion' can then be used to generate electricity as a 'regulated' flow of current.

The other obvious alternative is to pump water uphill whilst wind turbines or solar panels are generating power, then release the water at a steady flow rate as with a hydro-electric generating system, but Valleys are expensive!

Wind turbines and solar panels produce sporadic unregulated power in varying unpredictable magnitudes when located in inappropriate locations to which they are not entirely suited; therefore, their power output needs regulation before it becomes useful which adds significantly to the actual cost of employing them!

Wind Turbines & Storage of the Generated Electricity

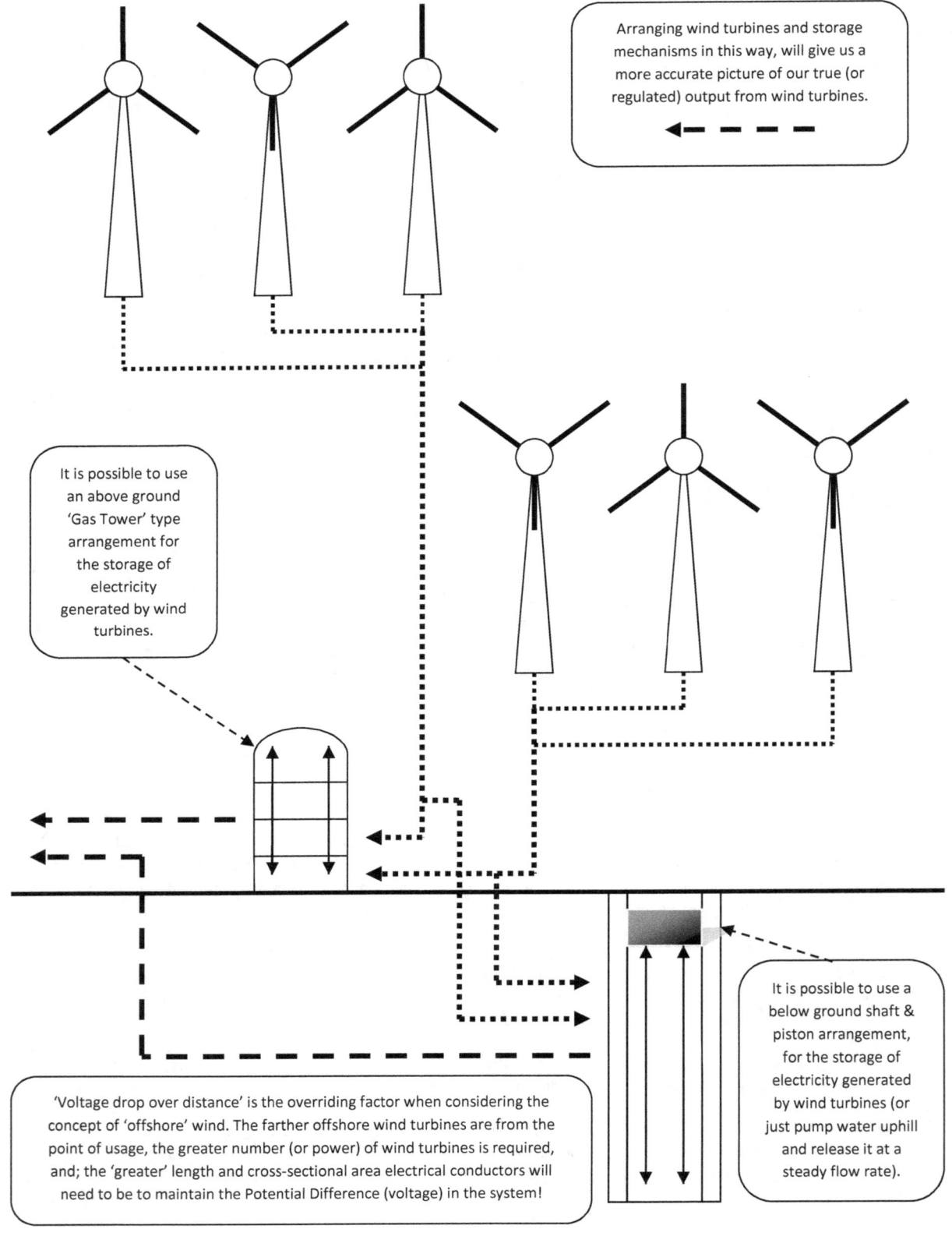

Arranging wind turbines and storage mechanisms in this way, will give us a more accurate picture of our true (or regulated) output from wind turbines.

It is possible to use an above ground 'Gas Tower' type arrangement for the storage of electricity generated by wind turbines.

It is possible to use a below ground shaft & piston arrangement, for the storage of electricity generated by wind turbines (or just pump water uphill and release it at a steady flow rate).

'Voltage drop over distance' is the overriding factor when considering the concept of 'offshore' wind. The farther offshore wind turbines are from the point of usage, the greater number (or power) of wind turbines is required, and; the 'greater' length and cross-sectional area electrical conductors will need to be to maintain the Potential Difference (voltage) in the system!

"Spitfire on a Stick" Independent, Seamless Tidal-stream Electricity Generator

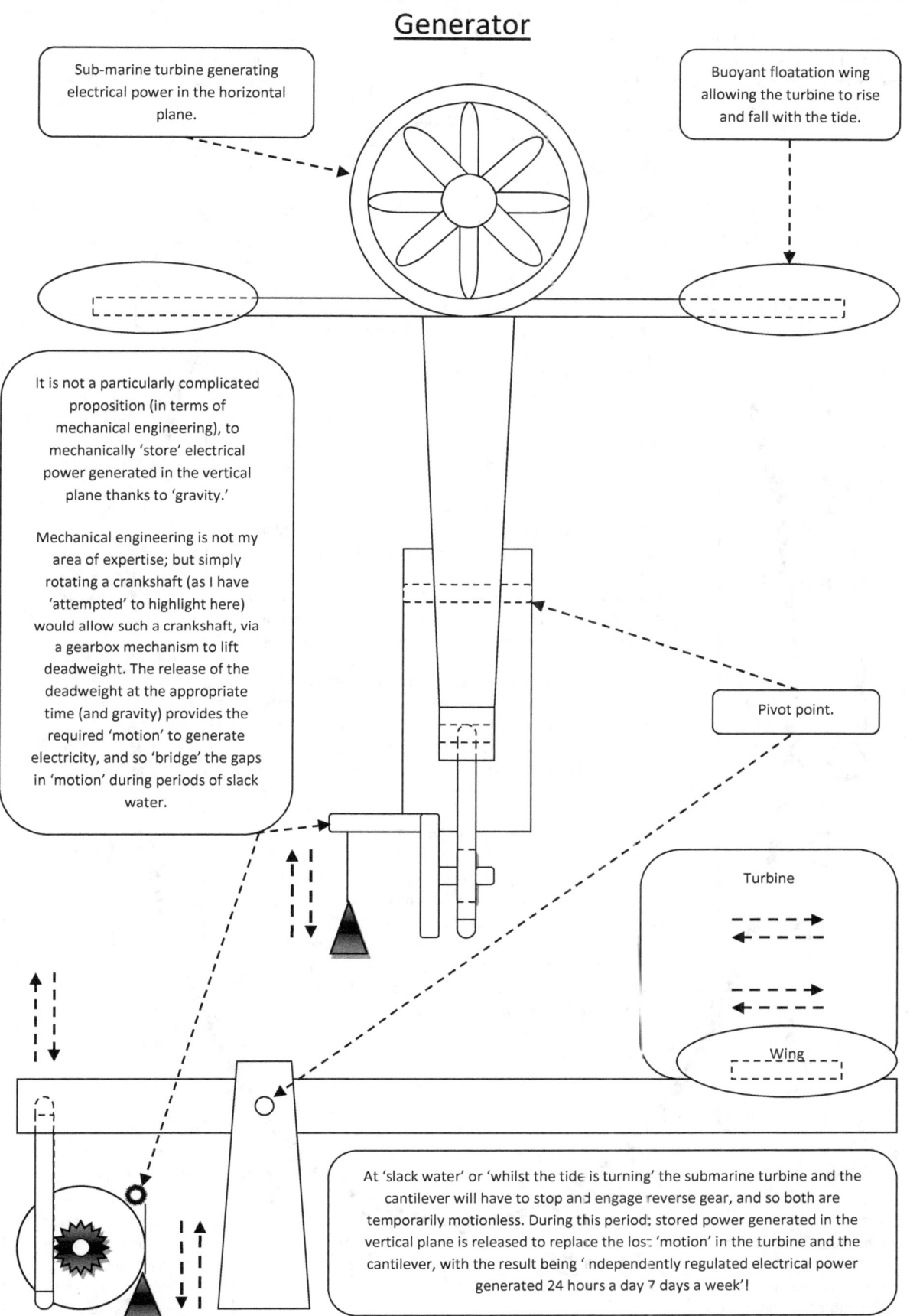

Sub-marine turbine generating electrical power in the horizontal plane.

Buoyant floatation wing allowing the turbine to rise and fall with the tide.

It is not a particularly complicated proposition (in terms of mechanical engineering), to mechanically 'store' electrical power generated in the vertical plane thanks to 'gravity.'

Mechanical engineering is not my area of expertise; but simply rotating a crankshaft (as I have 'attempted' to highlight here) would allow such a crankshaft, via a gearbox mechanism to lift deadweight. The release of the deadweight at the appropriate time (and gravity) provides the required 'motion' to generate electricity, and so 'bridge' the gaps in 'motion' during periods of slack water.

Pivot point.

Turbine

Wing

At 'slack water' or 'whilst the tide is turning' the submarine turbine and the cantilever will have to stop and engage reverse gear, and so both are temporarily motionless. During this period; stored power generated in the vertical plane is released to replace the lost 'motion' in the turbine and the cantilever, with the result being 'independently regulated electrical power generated 24 hours a day 7 days a week'!

Tidal-stream Electricity Generation & Temperature Controlled Distribution

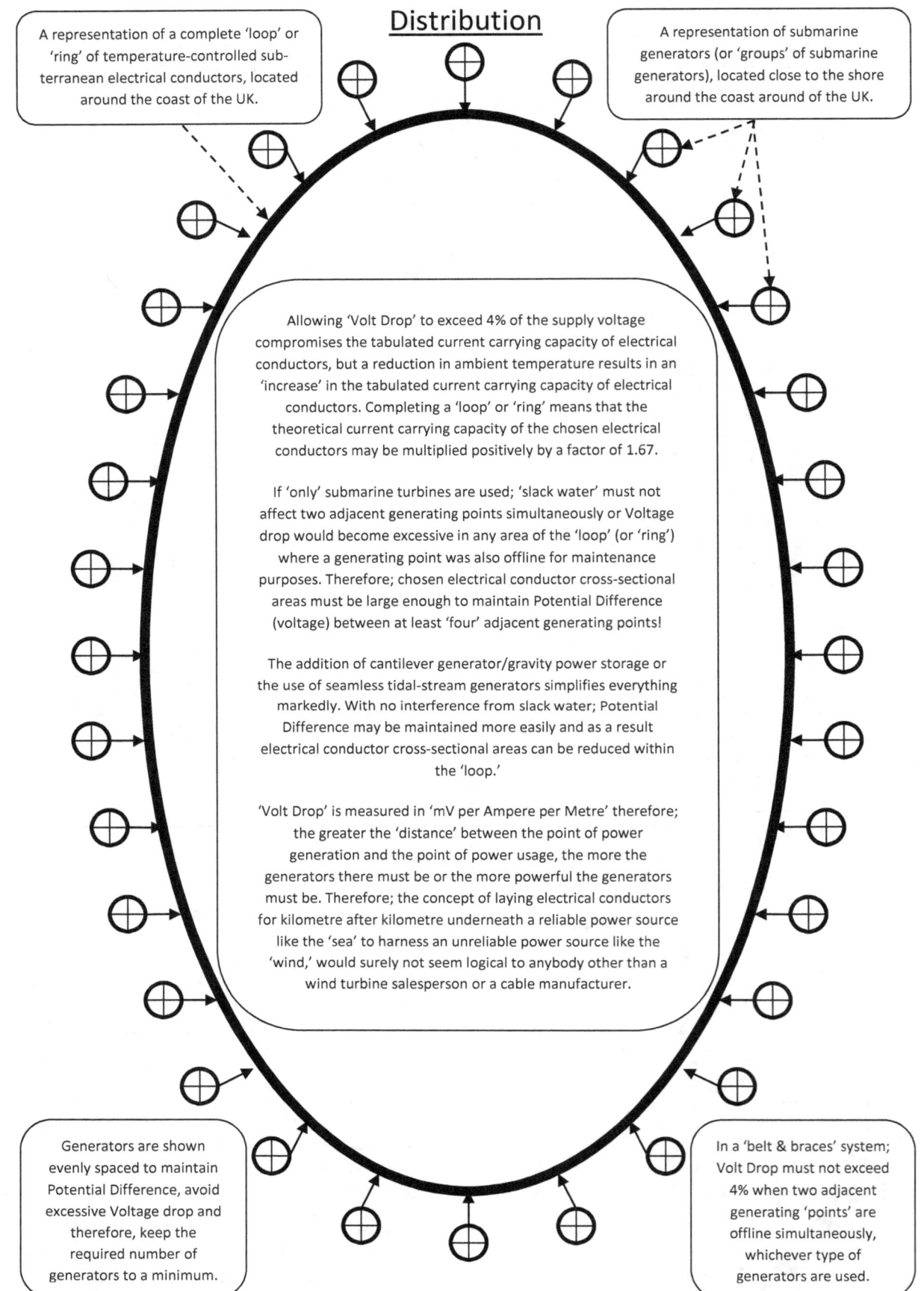

A representation of a complete 'loop' or 'ring' of temperature-controlled sub-terranean electrical conductors, located around the coast of the UK.

A representation of submarine generators (or 'groups' of submarine generators), located close to the shore around the coast around of the UK.

Allowing 'Volt Drop' to exceed 4% of the supply voltage compromises the tabulated current carrying capacity of electrical conductors, but a reduction in ambient temperature results in an 'increase' in the tabulated current carrying capacity of electrical conductors. Completing a 'loop' or 'ring' means that the theoretical current carrying capacity of the chosen electrical conductors may be multiplied positively by a factor of 1.67.

If 'only' submarine turbines are used; 'slack water' must not affect two adjacent generating points simultaneously or Voltage drop would become excessive in any area of the 'loop' (or 'ring') where a generating point was also offline for maintenance purposes. Therefore; chosen electrical conductor cross-sectional areas must be large enough to maintain Potential Difference (voltage) between at least 'four' adjacent generating points!

The addition of cantilever generator/gravity power storage or the use of seamless tidal-stream generators simplifies everything markedly. With no interference from slack water; Potential Difference may be maintained more easily and as a result electrical conductor cross-sectional areas can be reduced within the 'loop.'

'Volt Drop' is measured in 'mV per Ampere per Metre' therefore; the greater the 'distance' between the point of power generation and the point of power usage, the more the generators there must be or the more powerful the generators must be. Therefore; the concept of laying electrical conductors for kilometre after kilometre underneath a reliable power source like the 'sea' to harness an unreliable power source like the 'wind,' would surely not seem logical to anybody other than a wind turbine salesperson or a cable manufacturer.

Generators are shown evenly spaced to maintain Potential Difference, avoid excessive Voltage drop and therefore, keep the required number of generators to a minimum.

In a 'belt & braces' system; Volt Drop must not exceed 4% when two adjacent generating 'points' are offline simultaneously, whichever type of generators are used.

Temperature-Controlled Subterranean Distribution

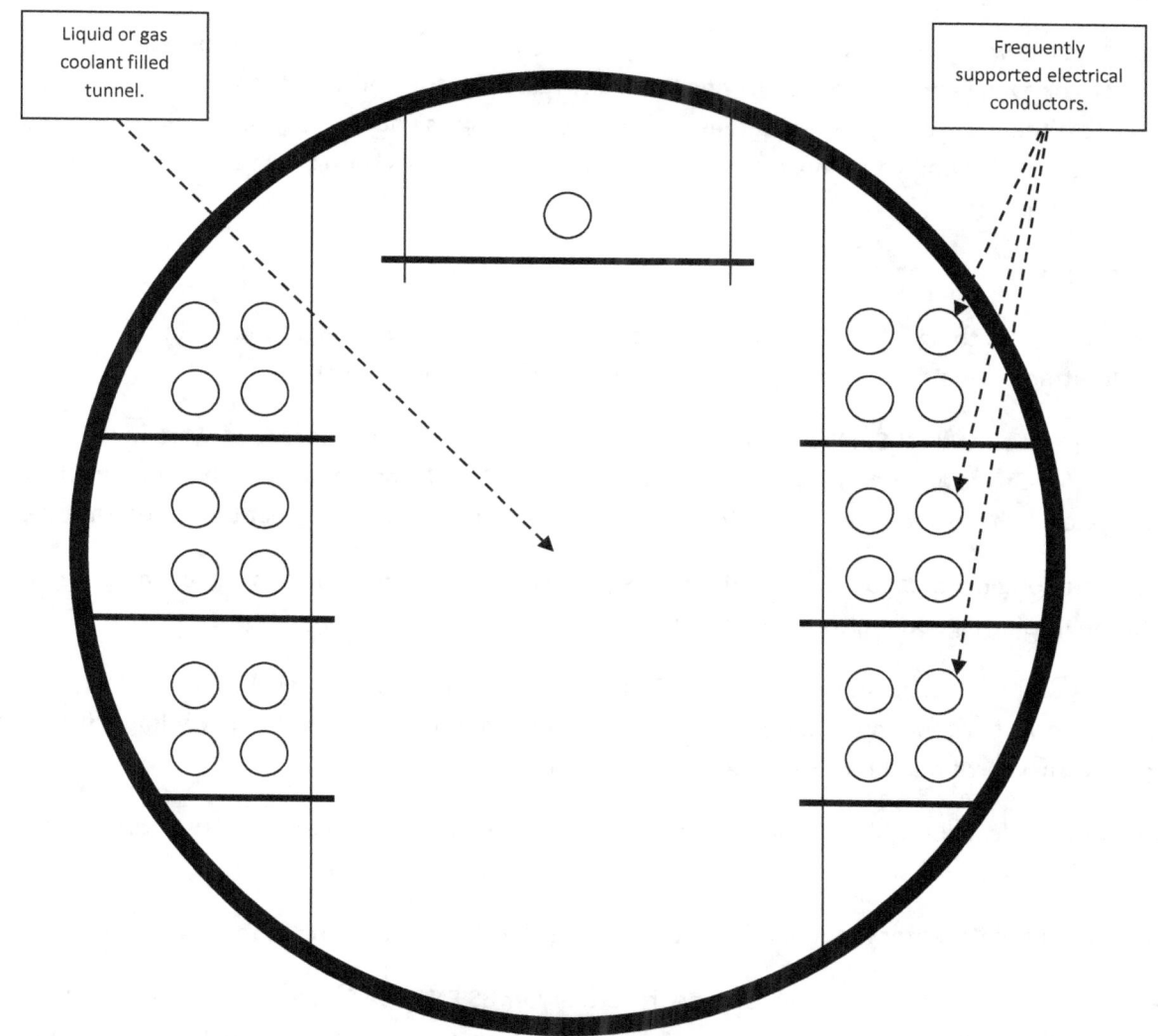

| Liquid or gas coolant filled tunnel. | | Frequently supported electrical conductors. |

There are 'two' distinct advantages to burying National Grid electrical power distribution system conductors underground:

(I) – The ambient temperature of the tunnel housing the electrical conductors can be controlled using gas or liquid cooling.

(ii) – The electrical conductors do not need to support their own weight over long distances; therefore, the physical construction of the electrical conductors can focus on the lowering of electrical resistance rather than the addition of physical strength.

Therefore; 'subterranean' electrical conductors of a smaller cross-sectional area can carry as much current as 'air cooled' electrical conductors of a greater cross-sectional area and; if the subterranean electrical conductors should reach their maximum tabulated current carrying capacity for any reason, the ambient temperature of the tunnel can be reduced with a liquid or gas coolant, which will effectively 'increase' the tabulated current carrying capacity of those subterranean electrical conductors.

Testing of Low Voltage (<500v ac) Electrical Installations

I think the easiest way to teach an inexperienced electrician about the testing of an electrical installation is to go through an appropriate testing Installation Schedule (replicated on the final page of this book) one column at a time.

Don't be too worried or nervous about testing an electrical installation because sometimes it can be months or even years in between having to do any testing of this sort and each time that you go back to it there are always a few nerves jangling, but as long as you have an appropriate Installation Schedule to fill in and you simply start at the beginning the nerves soon settle and it becomes really quite interesting.

Therefore:

Start with something nice and easy just to make sure your pen is working, by filling in the name of the Contractor, the date, your signature, and the address of the installation:

#1 – Type of supply TN-S TN-C-S TT; simply put a ring around whichever type of system you are testing; TN-S; line and neutral with a separate earth, TN-C-S; line and neutral with a combined and separate earth (also referred to as PME) or TT; a line and neutral system reliant on an earth stake.

#2 – Ze at origin.............ohms; record the external earth resistance value, this can be measured in ohms (Ω) using a good multi-meter or requested from the local electricity supplier.

#3 – PSCC......................kA; record the PSCC (prospective short circuit current) value, this can be measured with a good multi-meter or calculated using 'ohms law' with the supply voltage divided by the external earth resistance value (#2 – Ze ohms Ω).

#4 – Circuit; describe which circuit you are testing - cooker, shower, general purpose socket outlets, lighting?

#5 – no. of points; enter the number of outlets or light fittings on the circuit.

#6 – Over-current protective device: Type; record either BS EN Type B, C or D/ or BS Type 1, 2 or 3, MCB (miniature circuit breaker) or BS 3036 or 88 rewire-able/cartridge fuse. The first consideration when deciding on the '#6 - Type' and '#7 - nominal current rating' of an over-current protective device, is that the chosen device must efficiently protect the circuits' cabling from a **small overload of a long duration.**'

#7 – Over-current protective device: Rating Amps; record the nominal current value written on the front of the MCB, or current value of the fuse 'element' (cartridge or wire) which may be less than the 'maximum' rated current value written on the front of the fuse 'carrier'.

#8 – Over-current protective device: Breaking capacity kA; record the short circuit breaking capacity which should be written somewhere on the body of any over-current protective device, and; must exceed the 'prospective short circuit current value' (#3 - PSCC) of the system for the overcurrent protective device to be robust enough for the application.

#9 – Cable: Size mm²; record the cross-sectional area of the line and neutral conductors being protected.

#10 – Cable: CPC size mm²; record the cross-sectional area of the circuit protective conductor being protected.

#11 – Cable: Length m; the route taken by a circuits' cabling it is not always obvious, so it is sometimes a clever idea to make a note of your estimation of the 'length' of a circuit on a separate piece of paper before recording on the Installation Schedule (or have Tipp-ex handy).

Next; you should identify the test equipment you will be using, check that it is working, then test for continuity from the main earthing point of the building to all the extraneous-conductive-parts within the installation.

For the sake of clarity; an extraneous-conductive-part is:

"A conductive part liable to introduce a potential, generally earth potential, and not forming a part of the electrical installation." – Therefore:

All conductive parts of a building are 'liable to introduce a potential' of 230-240v if contacted by a line conductor such a damaged trailing flex or extension lead. The conductive parts within a building that are 'not forming a part of the electrical installation' are 'generally;' gas systems, water systems and structural steelwork; with the gas inside gas systems 'introducing earth potential,' the water inside water systems 'introducing earth potential,' and; the structural steelwork of the building concreted or bolted to the ground and therefore also 'introducing earth potential'!

Once continuity is confirmed across the completed earthing system:

You can be confident that if any damaged trailing flex or extension lead should contact any extraneous-conductive-part within an installation; it will cause a fault of negligible impedance to earth and the electricity supply will be automatically disconnected within the Regulation standard <0.4 of a second, rather than causing the extraneous-conductive-part to be energized (become 'hazardous' live) and provide an alternative (uncontrollable) route for electrical current to escape to the mass of the earth unused!

Next; <u>make sure the power is switched 'off'</u> and start testing circuit conductors:

#12 & #13 – Continuity: R1 + R2Ω & R2Ω; if you are on your own the easiest way to carry out this test is by bridging the conductors at the distribution board and taking measurements from each point, if there are two of you <u>(double check that the power switched is 'off' because;)</u> it is easier for one of you to take measurements at the distribution board whilst the other one bridges the conductors at each point.

To calculate R1 + R2Ω values accurately, and; to find any loose connections or badly warn switches or socket outlets, it is necessary to measure resistance in ohms (Ω) and make a note of the continuity values of all the conductors in a circuit whilst finding and rectifying any problems as you go along. The 'highest' measured and calculated values must be recorded for each circuit tested.

In a healthy 'power' circuit; the resistance values of the line (R1Ω) and the neutral conductors (being the same length and cross-sectional area) should be almost identical, if they are not, it suggests that there must be a loose connection somewhere along the length of one of the conductors. There should also be an easily recognisable relationship when comparing line and neutral conductor resistances with the circuit protective conductor (R2Ω) resistance, although the line and neutral and the circuit protective conductors may be of a different cross-sectional area, they are still of a similar length so the ratio between the two values should always reflect that fact with the larger cross-sectional area conductors having a consistently lower measured resistance than the smaller ones.

In a healthy 'lighting' circuit; the resistance values of the 'un-switched' line and neutral conductors (again being of the same length and cross-sectional area) should also be almost identical and with 1.0mm²/1.0mm² lighting cable the circuit protective conductor resistance will also be the same, if they are not you are once again looking for loose connections. Where the circuit protective conductor is of a smaller cross-sectional area than the live conductors as with 1.5mm²/1.0mm² lighting cables, there should (as with a power circuit) be an easily recognisable relationship between the 'un-switched' line and neutral conductors and the circuit protective conductor as once again, these conductors are of a similar length. The 'switched' line conductors will have measured resistance values that are greater than either the 'un-switched' line, neutral or circuit protective conductor measured resistance values as the 'switched' line conductor 'adds length' to the part of the circuit being tested.

When testing an older electrical system, it can be a clever idea to replace any 'well used' switches (particularly the 2way switches) & sockets outlets before you start.

As you test the 'continuity' of electrical conductors with the power supply switched 'off' this evaluation is with the cabling at 'room temperature,' therefore it is 'only during continuity testing' that any loose connections and badly warn light switches or socket outlets will be located. Failing to rectify any such problems will waste energy and eventually cause the circuit to break down! Once the power is switched 'on' and the circuit energized, live conductors become hot and expand to fill any gaps!

#14, #15 & #16 – Insulation Resistance: M Ω: Phase/Neutral, Phase/Earth, Neutral/Earth; *your test equipment produces 500v when conducting this test to ascertain whether the 'insulation' of any live conductors has been 'compromised' in any way, so take care!

Even though it is an acceptable Regulation standard to have measured insulation resistance values as low as 0.5M Ω, insulation resistance 'current leakage' with a measured value of as little as 4.0M Ω will 'increase current usage' across an entire electrical installation by approximately 30%! Therefore; although a 0.5M Ω insulation resistance fault is considered 'safe,' it cannot be considered 'efficient' and is going to increase current flow through your clients' electric meter by somewhere near 50%!

Also; replace any cabling within a domestic/light industrial/commercial electrical installation with a measured insulation resistance value that falls below >200M Ω because:

Did you ever try to take a drink of water directly from a cold tap as a kid and get your lips stuck to the tap?...........That was earth 'leakage' current!

Insulation resistance faults cause earth leakage current and earth leakage current will be noticeable on every earthed exposed-conductive-part and every earthed extraneous-conductive-part of any electrical installation where it is present. *If anybody is seriously hurt or killed because of removing or not installing safety earthing to exposed or extraneous-conductive parts, the legal responsibility/ liability is yours and yours alone, because; it is not possible to protect yourself in a Court of Law by presenting any document that has been legally disclaimed by its author!

High quality metering equipment will record up to >299M Ω, infinity (∞) is no longer an acceptable recorded insulation resistance value.

#17 – Earth Loop Impedance: ZT Ω; this test measures the 'total' impedance to the flow of earth fault current (ZT 'total' Ω) of a resistive 'loop' of conductors from the mass of the earth to the supply transformer, that includes; the supply line conductor (R1Ω), via a replicated fault of negligible impedance to earth, the circuit protective conductor (R2Ω), and; the 'external' earthing conductor(s) and electrode (Ze 'external' Ω).

Record the highest measured values, which will be from the point on a circuit that is furthest away from the distribution board. By the time 'continuity' and 'insulation resistance' have been tested and any problems have been observed, located, and resolved:

A measured earth fault loop impedance test value (ZT Ω) of less than the Regulation standard maximum tabulated value, will confirm a circuits' cabling has not exceeded the maximum length permissible to guarantee achieving the Regulation standard maximum <0.4 of a second automatic disconnection of supply time during a fault of negligible impedance to earth, and; not exceeded the Regulation standard maximum 4% 'Volt Drop'. Excessive voltage drop (>4% of the supply voltage) will cause the current usage of any circuit to increase simply because of Ohms Law, wasting power unnecessarily by causing an increase in conductor temperatures and escalating electricity bills as a result.

Measured with the power switched 'on,' and therefore with the circuit conductors at 'operating' temperature; an earth loop impedance (ZT Ω) value on its' own will not be of any use in spotting loose connections or badly warn switches and socket outlets, until such faults become very wasteful.

*Note: Once this test is completed; it becomes possible to cross reference 'earth loop impedance measurements,' 'continuity values' and 'cable lengths' right across your entire Installation Schedule, so therefore allowing you to make more accurate estimations of the length of any circuits that you were not too sure about earlier.

#18 & #19 - RCD: mA and mS; test from each point on each circuit at 50% of the tripping current of the device to make sure the device is not too sensitive, before testing from each point on each circuit again at the rated tripping current of the device to confirm a disconnection time. *Generally; 30mA RCDs protecting socket outlets, can then be tested at five times the tripping current of the device before recording a disconnection time.

RCD testing is really a test of function; being intended to ascertain whether a current imbalance of an unacceptable magnitude between line and neutral will cause the RCD to automatically disconnect the electricity supply via any/all protected outlets. this test will immediately determine whether anybody has cured 'nuisance tripping' of the RCD by spraying aerosol antiperspirant into the mechanism of the device (or by turning it upside down and filling it with sand in older devices). This test is particularly important because among other reasons; a dysfunctional RCD within an electrical system also lacking in safety earthing could if the planets align against you; result in a **gas explosion**!

You need to record the nominal tripping current of the RCD (#18) which in installations supplied by TN-S and TN-C-S systems is most likely to be 30mA, with TT system main switches more generally being 100/300/500/1000mA. You should record measured disconnection times (#19) of <40mS in the case of circuits supplying socket outlets, with readings of <200mS being acceptable for lighting circuits or 100/300/500/1000mA split-load distribution board main switches. A 30mA RCD must be protecting socket outlets intended to supply appliances for use outdoors, whilst indoors; installing a 30mA RCD is the best way of protecting against simultaneous contact with a line conductor and any part of your earthing system.

#20 – Polarity; if there have been no issues with regards to crossed polarity whilst performing any of the tests above, I think it will be safe to put a tick in this column.

#21 – Remarks; please remember that anybody having a difficult day can have a complete blind spot when trying to sort out a particularly tricky problem, so here you have a chance to make a note pointing to a separate sheet of paper explaining what you may have done. Anybody following you in or even you yourself on a better day, may well be able to go straight to the problem and sort it out in no time at all if prior knowledge is available.

#22 – Main bonding check: Gas; it is particularly important to check that the main gas bonding is in place because; you have no control at all over the state of trailing flexible cables and extension leads that occupants may use within the building. Any damaged/bared trailing flex or extension lead that comes close enough to a conductive part of a gas system will allow earth fault current to arc across, as the fault current will recognise a path back to the mass of the earth via the gas within the system. Controlling the speed of the automatic disconnection of the electrical supply is crucial in preventing a gas explosion and the cross-sectional area of the main gas bonding cable, effectively controls the speed at which you can divert fault current to the main earthing point of the installation and so therefore, achieve the Regulation standard maximum <0.4 of a second automatic disconnection of supply time during a fault of negligible impedance to earth.

#22 – Main bonding check: Water; as above; any damaged/bared trailing flex or extension lead that comes close enough to a conductive part of a water system will allow earth fault current to arc across, as the fault current will recognise a path back to the mass of the earth via the water within the system. Therefore, controlling the speed of automatic disconnection of supply becomes crucial in preventing conductive parts of the water system from becoming 'hazardous live' and providing an uncontrollable path for fault current to find a way back to the mass of the earth unused! It is again the cross-sectional area of the main water bonding conductor that controls the speed at which you can return fault current to the main earthing point of the installation and therefore, achieve the Regulation standard maximum <0.4 of a second automatic disconnection of supply time during a fault of negligible impedance to earth.

#22 – Main bonding check: Other; it is important to check that the structural steel work is earth bonded for similar reasons to '#22 - water,' whilst for incoming oil supplies the reason for checking would be somewhere in between the thinking for '#22 - gas and #22 - water.'

#22 – size.........mm²; the sizing of main bonding conductors is dependent upon the incoming supply characteristics of our installation, with TN-S, TN-C-S types of electricity supply requiring a cable of a minimum 10.0mm² cross sectional area and TT electricity supplies with an RCD main switch requiring a cable of a minimum 6.0mm² cross sectional area .

Due to the unreliability of '#2 - (Ze Ω)' provided by an earth stake in a TT system, the MCB's within the distribution board can only be relied upon for effective overcurrent protection, and; it is the 'RCD main switch' that is relied upon to achieve the Regulation standard maximum <0.4 of a second automatic disconnection of supply time during a fault of negligible impedance to earth. As an RCD can react ten times faster than an MCB (in just <40mS or <0.04 of a second), main earthing conductor cross-sectional areas in a TT supplied system can, as with the main bonding; be reduced to only 6.0mm².

#23- Main Earth size........mm²; the sizing of the Main Earth conductor in a TN-S or TN-C-S system is dependent upon the cross-sectional area of the incoming supply live conductors, therefore if the line and neutral have a cross-sectional area of 25mm², the main earthing conductor would be the next size down with a cross-sectional area of 16mm², whilst 35mm² live supply conductors would require a main earthing conductor of 25mm² etc. etc.

Due to the reliability of '#2 - (Ze Ω)' provided by the earthed central point of the supply transformer in a TN-S or TN-C-S system, the MCB's within the distribution board can be relied upon for effective overcurrent protection, and; to achieve the Regulation standard maximum <0.4 of a second automatic disconnection of supply time during a fault of negligible impedance to earth!

#24 – Earth Electrical Resistance.............Ω; the Earth Electrical Resistance of an electrical installation should be very slightly lower than the '#2 – Ze Ω' resistance value recorded earlier on. The difference between these two resistance values being that the '#2 – Ze Ω' value is a measurement of the resistance from the distribution board to the earthed centre point of the supply transformer (or the earth stake), whilst the value of the 'earth electrical resistance' of the installation is effectively reduced by including separate paths to the mass of the earth via incoming gas and water supplies and/or the structural steel work of a building. *Climatic conditions have the habit of interfering with these two values whilst you try to measure them and with the two being so close together; you may find yourself connecting and disconnecting main bonding cables once or twice before getting these two values around the right way.

Deviations from Wiring Regulations and Special Notes; in 1991 when the Electrical Wiring Regulations earned the title "BS 7671", full compliance with them meant that people or livestock could only be killed or very badly hurt through human error. Therefore, to drop below the safety and efficiency standards of those regulations must also be 'human error'!

*Now that the UK can afford to do so, just adding "the protection of all trailing flexes and extension leads by a 30mA RCD" to the 1991 Electrical Wiring Regulations; makes those regulations the perfect (legally compliant) electrical safety and efficiency standards for today.

Time Current Characteristics – Large overload of a Short Duration

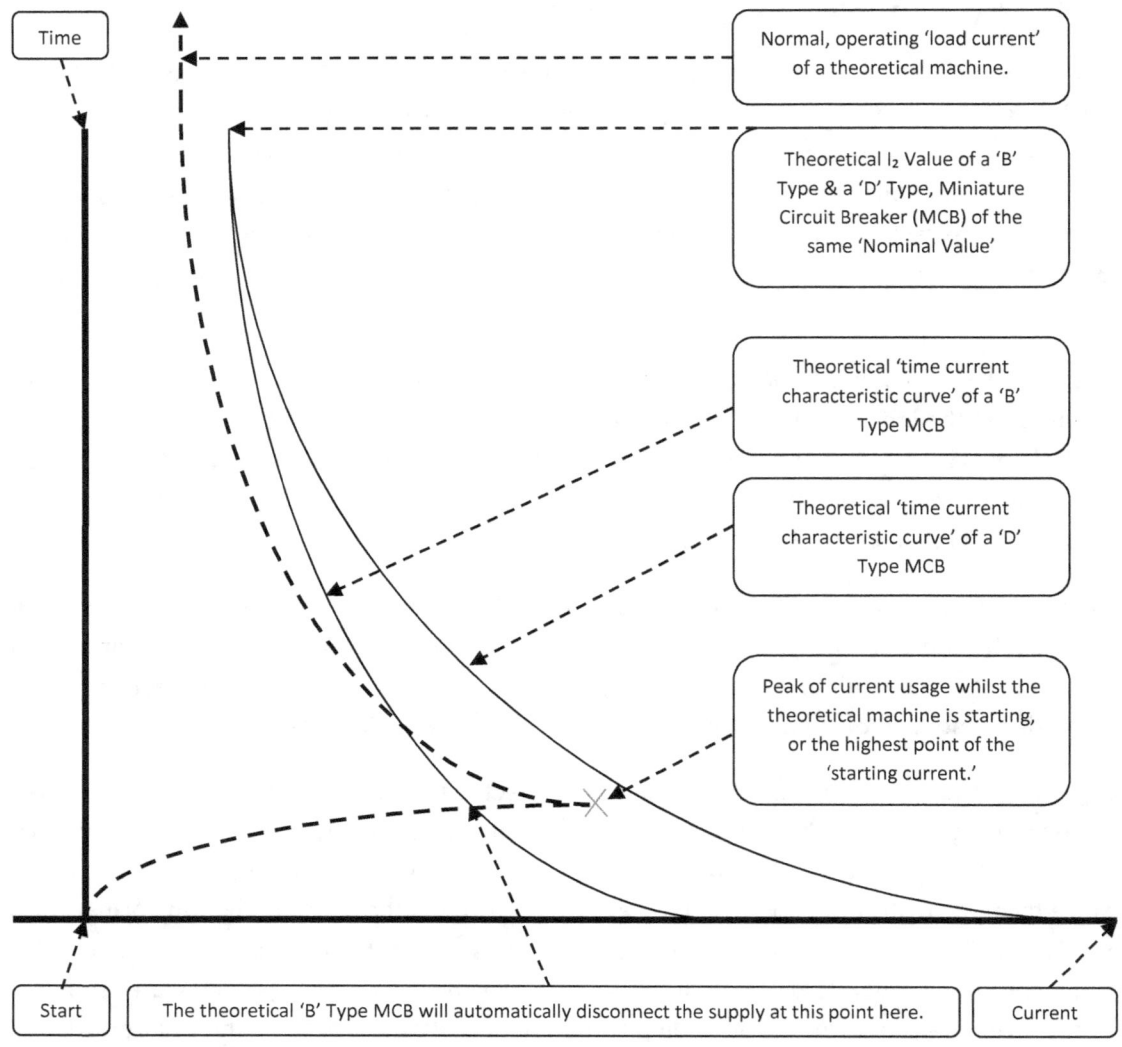

Time

Normal, operating 'load current' of a theoretical machine.

Theoretical I₂ Value of a 'B' Type & a 'D' Type, Miniature Circuit Breaker (MCB) of the same 'Nominal Value'

Theoretical 'time current characteristic curve' of a 'B' Type MCB

Theoretical 'time current characteristic curve' of a 'D' Type MCB

Peak of current usage whilst the theoretical machine is starting, or the highest point of the 'starting current.'

Start

The theoretical 'B' Type MCB will automatically disconnect the supply at this point here.

Current

As you can see if you study the drawing above; machine rated miniature circuit breakers such as BS EN Type 'C' or 'D' or BS Type '2' or '3' versions, will be capable of absorbing any high starting currents associated with large (usually) rotating machines. The use of a 'fusing factor' of 1.45 will allow for the use of a BS EN Type 'B' or BS Type '1' miniature circuit breaker of a greater 'nominal value,' as you may well have one kicking about in the shed or even in the back of the van, but this is only used (generally speaking) as a 'temporary' measure until an appropriate machine rated miniature circuit breaker can be located.

A fusing factor of 1.45 may be a part of your equation where atmospheric conditions restrict you to the use of a 'fuse' as your chosen over-current protective device, with the fusing factor effectively 'bridging any gaps' between any two available fuse element sizes. An in-series amp-meter would ideally be a permanent part of any circuit where a fusing factor is used, to protect that circuit from 'small overloads of a long duration' by permanently monitoring the current flow within that circuit.

Time Current Characteristics – Small overload of a Long Duration

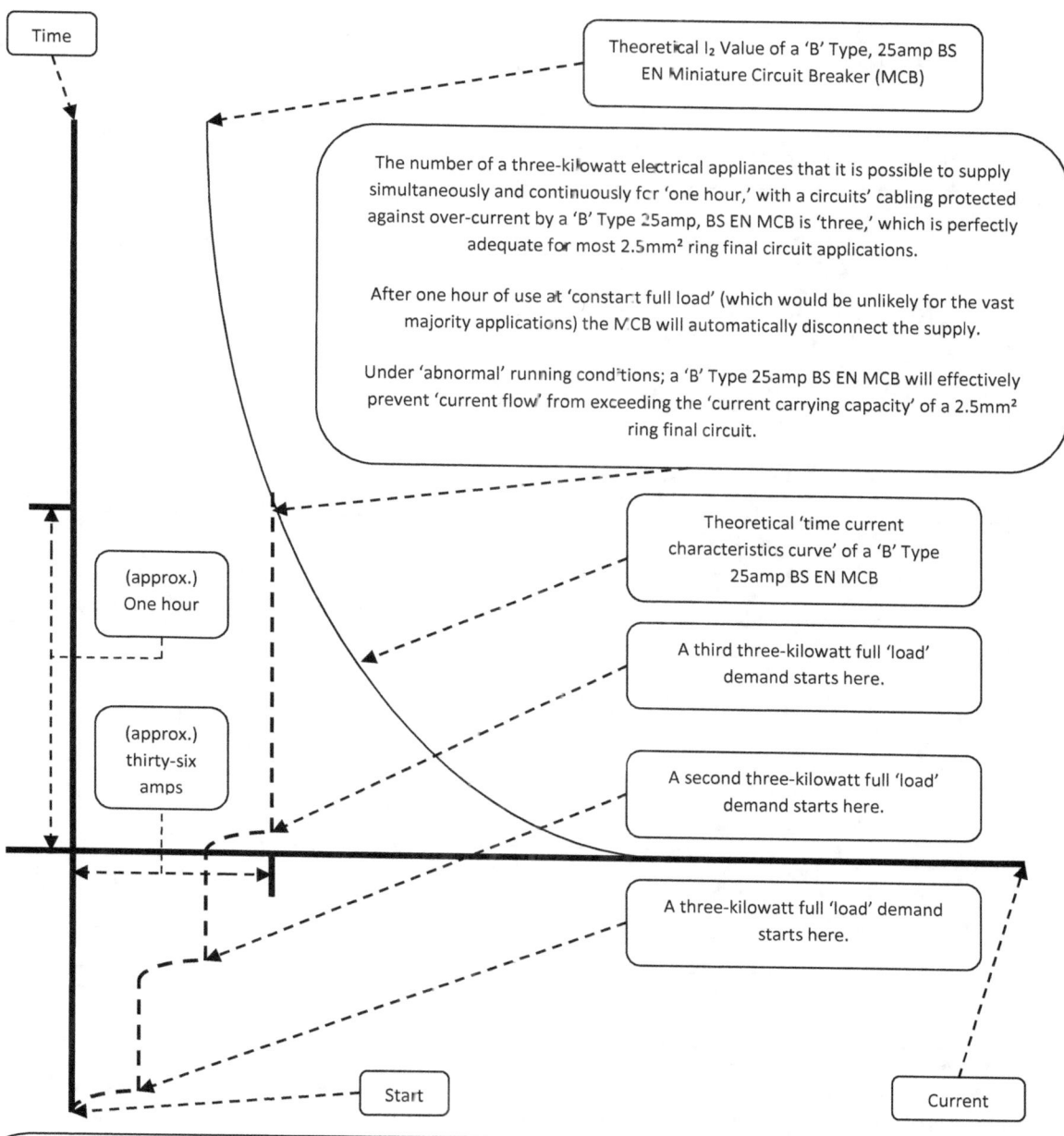

Time

Theoretical I_2 Value of a 'B' Type, 25amp BS EN Miniature Circuit Breaker (MCB)

The number of a three-kilowatt electrical appliances that it is possible to supply simultaneously and continuously for 'one hour,' with a circuits' cabling protected against over-current by a 'B' Type 25amp, BS EN MCB is 'three,' which is perfectly adequate for most 2.5mm² ring final circuit applications.

After one hour of use at 'constant full load' (which would be unlikely for the vast majority applications) the MCB will automatically disconnect the supply.

Under 'abnormal' running conditions; a 'B' Type 25amp BS EN MCB will effectively prevent 'current flow' from exceeding the 'current carrying capacity' of a 2.5mm² ring final circuit.

(approx.) One hour

(approx.) thirty-six amps

Theoretical 'time current characteristics curve' of a 'B' Type 25amp BS EN MCB

A third three-kilowatt full 'load' demand starts here.

A second three-kilowatt full 'load' demand starts here.

A three-kilowatt full 'load' demand starts here.

Start

Current

Unless 'all' the general-purpose socket outlets supplied by a power circuit are intended to be switched on simultaneously; the 'load current' demand on such a circuit is restricted to a maximum of one 13amp appliance applying a current demand at a time, so it is not possible to subject a general-purpose socket outlet circuit to a 'large overload of a short duration'.

An overcurrent protective device must therefore effectively protect general-purpose socket outlet circuits against 'small overloads of a long duration' for when appliances or the circuits' cabling is damaged, faulty, or abused. When the current carrying capacity of the chosen cable exceeds the I2 value of the overcurrent protective device, overcurrent protection is effective and faulty, wasteful appliances or circuit cabling, 'correctly'; become un-usable.

Continuity of a Lighting Circuit

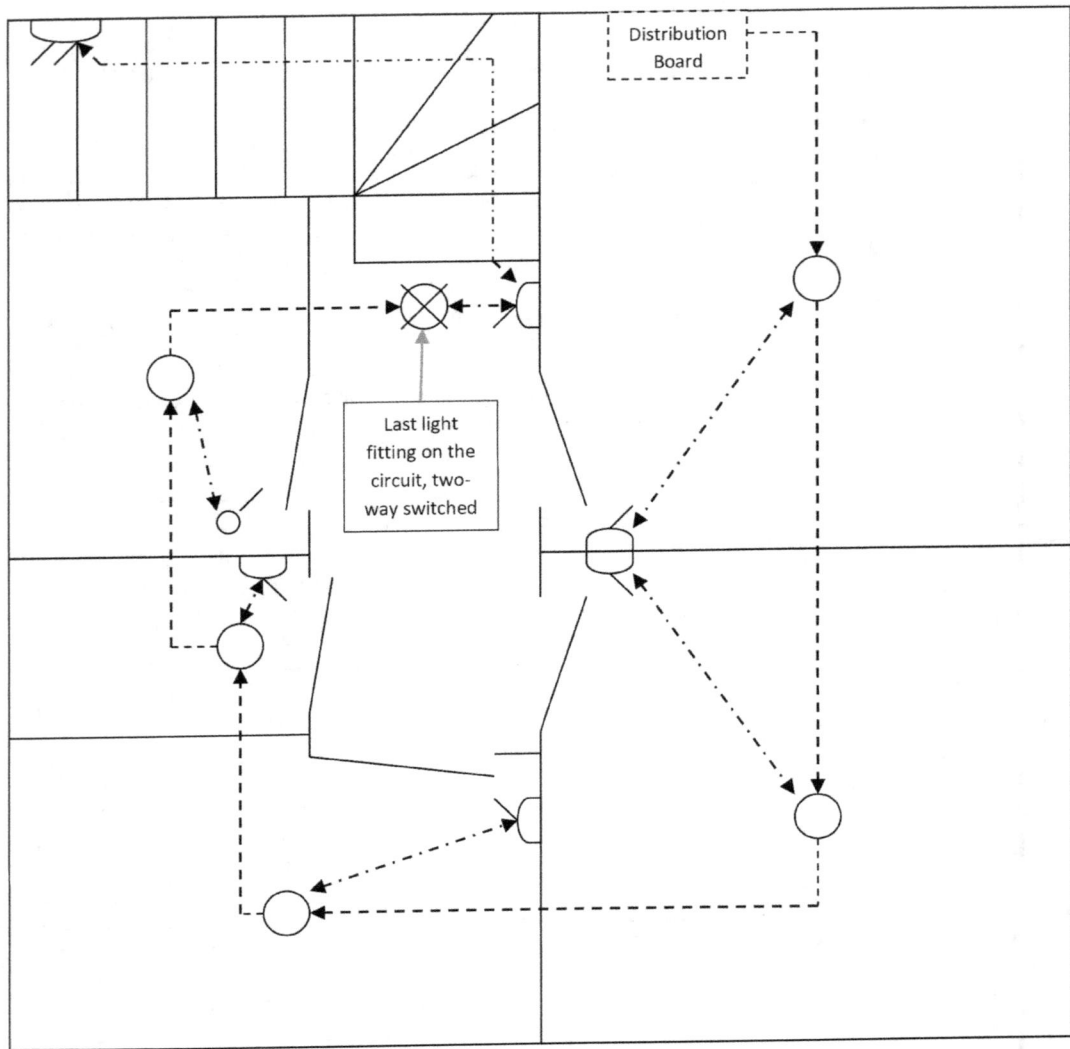

Distribution Board

Last light fitting on the circuit, two-way switched

You should conduct the continuity testing of a lighting circuit from every light fitting on that circuit. With the power switched 'off;' connect or 'bridge' the conductors so that the further you are away from the distribution board, the greater the measured resistance values will become. This allows you to ascertain which is the light fitting on the circuit furthest away from the distribution board and to then record the highest measured values onto your Installation Schedule. In a domestic installation the 'highest' measured values would usually be from/to a light fitting controlled by a two-way switch, as the 'strapping' cables of that two-way switch are a part of the continuity test. The measured neutral, 'un-switched' line and circuit protective conductor values should all have a recognisable relationship between them if the conductors are 1.5mm²/1.0mm², or all be equal if the conductors are 1.0mm²/1.0mm² or 1.5mm²/1.5mm², the longer 'switched' line conductor values should always be higher. Where no metal-clad switches are involved; not wanting to disturb the decor will result in the continuity of the circuit protective conductor from the light fitting to the switch, becoming irrelevant for continuity testing purposes.

Comparing all measured values (line, neutral and circuit protective conductor); will allow you to spot loose connections and/or warn out switches as you go along and provide an opportunity for you to rectify any problems, before finally measuring and calculating, then recording the R1 + R2Ω and R2Ω values onto your Installation Schedule.

As you conduct continuity testing at room temperature with the power switched 'off;' any loose connections and/or warn out switches in a circuit, will result in noticeably high measured resistance values compared to other parts of that circuit or other similar circuits.

Continuity of a Power Circuit

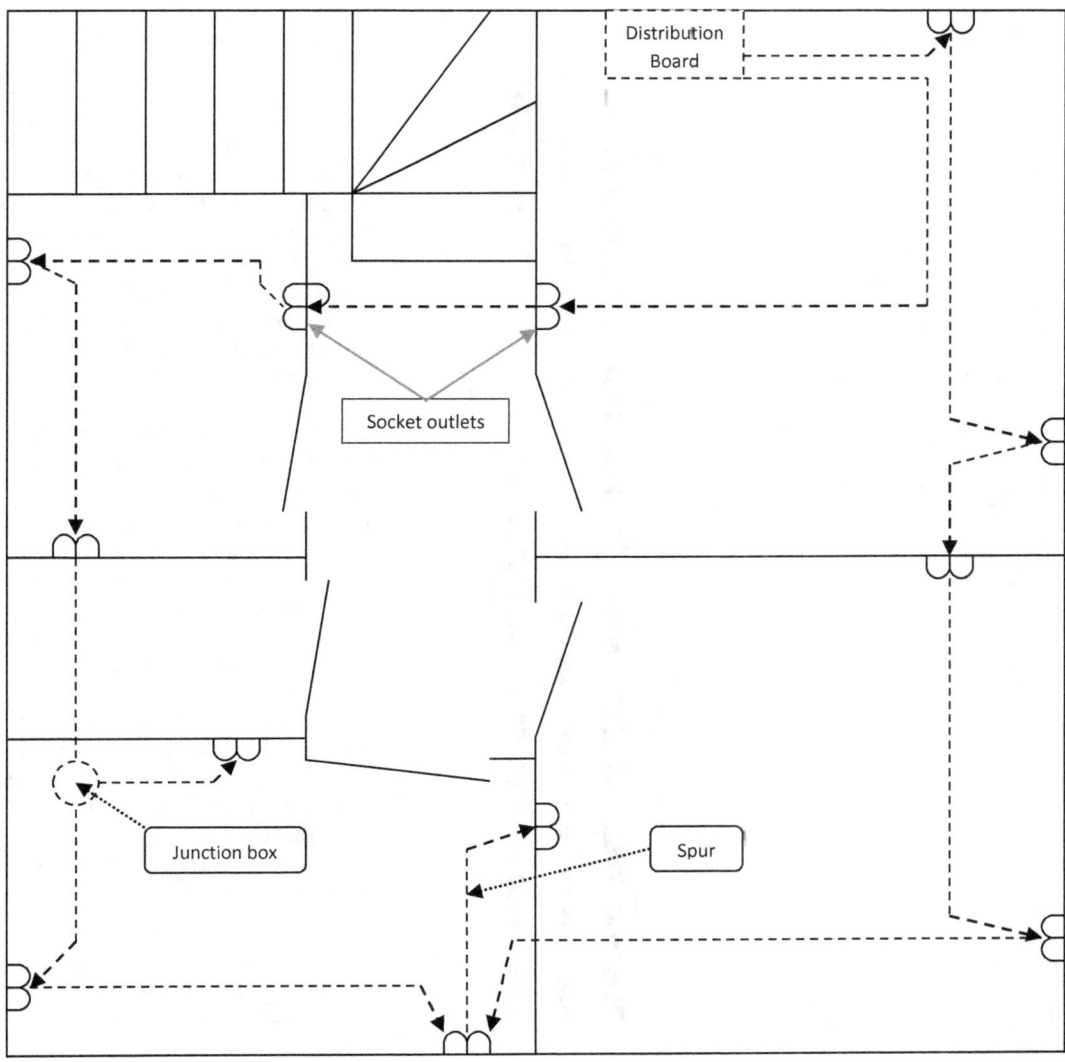

You conduct the continuity testing of a power circuit from every outlet on that circuit. With the power switched 'off;' connect or 'bridge' the conductors so that the further you are away from the distribution board, the greater the measured resistance values will become. This allows you to ascertain which outlet represents the point that is furthest away from the distribution board, then you can record these 'highest measured values' from/to that outlet. In the example above the measured (and calculated) values from the 'spurred' socket outlet are likely to be the highest, and; would therefore be the values recorded as representing R1 + R2Ω and R2Ω.

Comparing the recorded values of a final ring circuits' line and neutral conductors should show measured values that are equal, the ratio between line and neutral conductor values and circuit protective conductor values should be easily recognisable whether the cabling is 2.5mm²/1.5mm² or 4.0mm²/1.5mm². If measured values of line and neutral conductors are unequal, or equal line and neutral conductor values compared to circuit protective conductor values appear to be in a strange ratio, it will certainly be because of loose connections or badly warn socket outlets. If you choose a BS EN 32amp MCB to protect a 4.0mm²/1.5mm² ring final circuit from over-current; only the use of 'earthed metal-clad' socket fronts will ensure a safe automatic disconnection of supply time, if a 'wrapped fuse' should cause a 13amp plug line pin to overheat.

You conduct continuity testing at room temperature with the power switched 'off,' so any loose connections and/or badly warn socket outlets in a circuit, will result in noticeably high measured resistance values.

Insulation Resistance

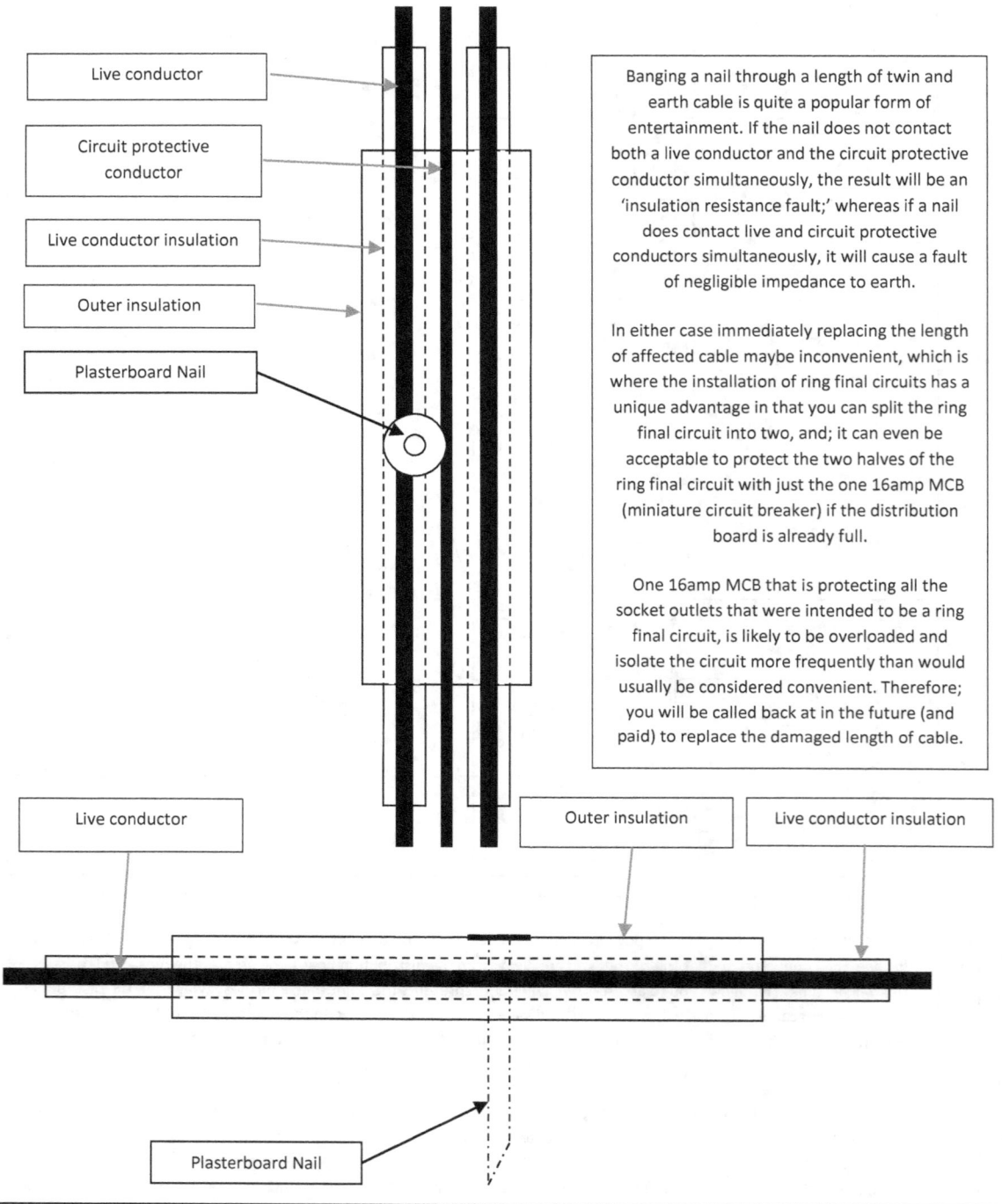

Live conductor

Circuit protective conductor

Live conductor insulation

Outer insulation

Plasterboard Nail

Banging a nail through a length of twin and earth cable is quite a popular form of entertainment. If the nail does not contact both a live conductor and the circuit protective conductor simultaneously, the result will be an 'insulation resistance fault;' whereas if a nail does contact live and circuit protective conductors simultaneously, it will cause a fault of negligible impedance to earth.

In either case immediately replacing the length of affected cable maybe inconvenient, which is where the installation of ring final circuits has a unique advantage in that you can split the ring final circuit into two, and; it can even be acceptable to protect the two halves of the ring final circuit with just the one 16amp MCB (miniature circuit breaker) if the distribution board is already full.

One 16amp MCB that is protecting all the socket outlets that were intended to be a ring final circuit, is likely to be overloaded and isolate the circuit more frequently than would usually be considered convenient. Therefore; you will be called back at in the future (and paid) to replace the damaged length of cable.

Live conductor

Outer insulation

Live conductor insulation

Plasterboard Nail

A nail does not actually have to encounter two electrical conductors simultaneously to cause an insulation resistance fault and for that insulation resistance fault to be intrusive enough to result in 'nuisance tripping' of an RCD (residual current device) 'under load,' all the nails must do is compromise the live conductors' insulation. Once the load current demand on a length of affected cable is of a relevant magnitude, nuisance tripping of the RCD will be the first obvious evidence of the insulation resistance fault being a problem within the affected circuit. The amplification of load current demand across the entire affected electrical system caused by any insulation resistance fault, which could rise to 30/40 or even 50%, may happen gradually enough to go un-noticed by the person paying the electric bill!

Insulation Resistance #2

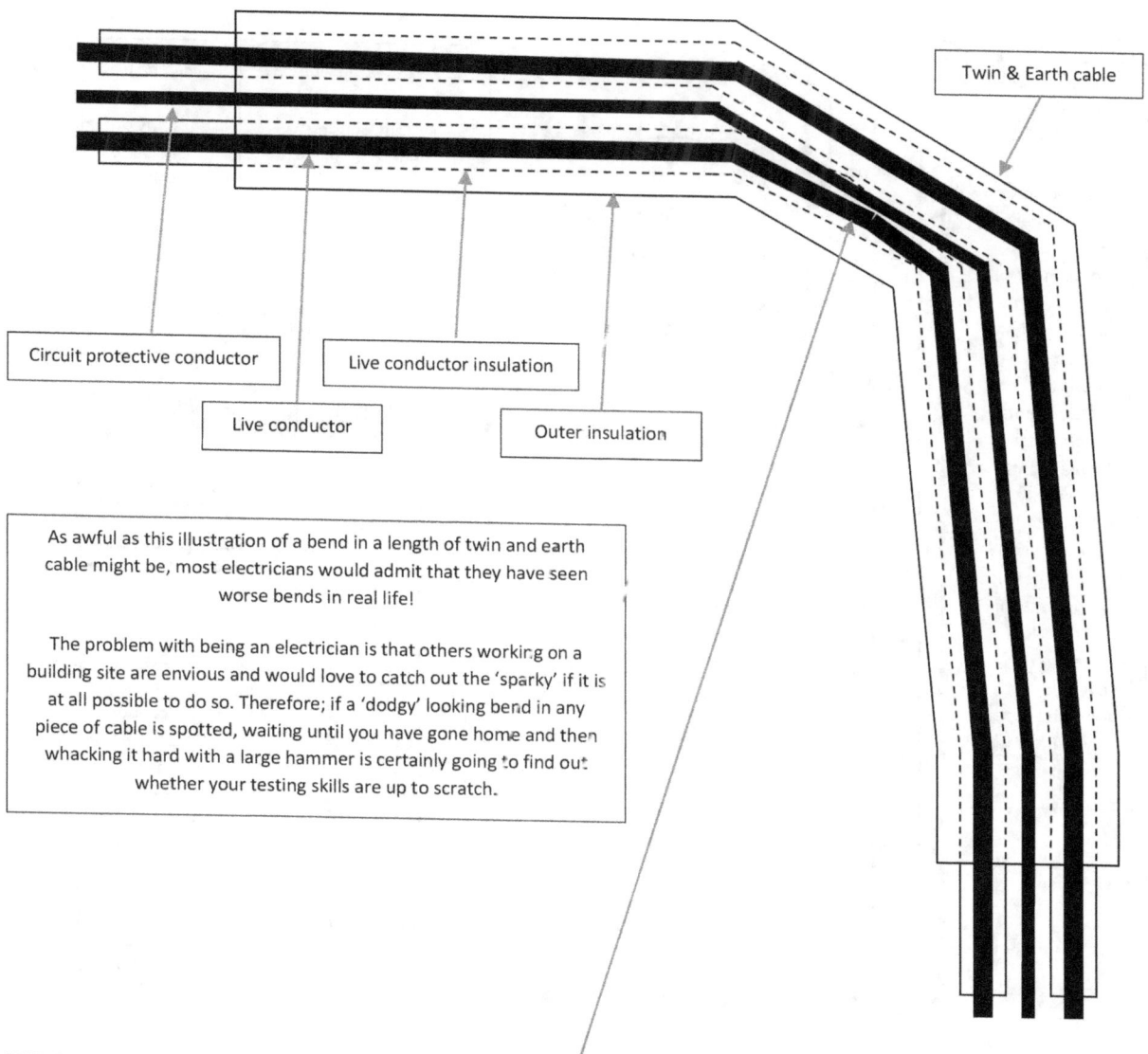

Twin & Earth cable

Circuit protective conductor

Live conductor insulation

Live conductor

Outer insulation

As awful as this illustration of a bend in a length of twin and earth cable might be, most electricians would admit that they have seen worse bends in real life!

The problem with being an electrician is that others working on a building site are envious and would love to catch out the 'sparky' if it is at all possible to do so. Therefore; if a 'dodgy' looking bend in any piece of cable is spotted, waiting until you have gone home and then whacking it hard with a large hammer is certainly going to find out whether your testing skills are up to scratch.

Nuisance Tripping – Automatic Disconnection of Supply

Conductors do not have to be in direct contact to cause 'nuisance tripping' of a residual current device (RCD):

Live conductor 'insulation' crushed into a circuit protective conductor in this way will be compromised or even split, causing earth 'leakage' current and then eventually earth 'fault' current to pass between conductors once load current demand reaches the appropriate magnitudes.

The amplification of the load current demand caused by an insulation resistance fault, increases the speed at which that fault will deteriorate therefore; effectively 'spiralling' the problem. The problem will at first represent earth 'leakage' current; causing nuisance tripping of the RCD and an amplification of current usage at the electric meter, then the problem will degrade into something representing earth 'fault' current; causing the automatic disconnection of the electricity supply by overloading the appropriate over-current protective device (miniature circuit breaker or fuse). Which overcurrent protective device will automatically disconnect the supply is dependent upon whether the fault is between 'neutral' and circuit protective conductors; which will rupture the cartridge fuse located within the 13amp plug, or between 'line' and circuit protective conductors; which will trip the MCB or rupture the fuse element (cartridge or wire) within a fuse carrier, located within the distribution board.

Insulation Resistance Faults and Their Relationship with an Increased Load Current Demand

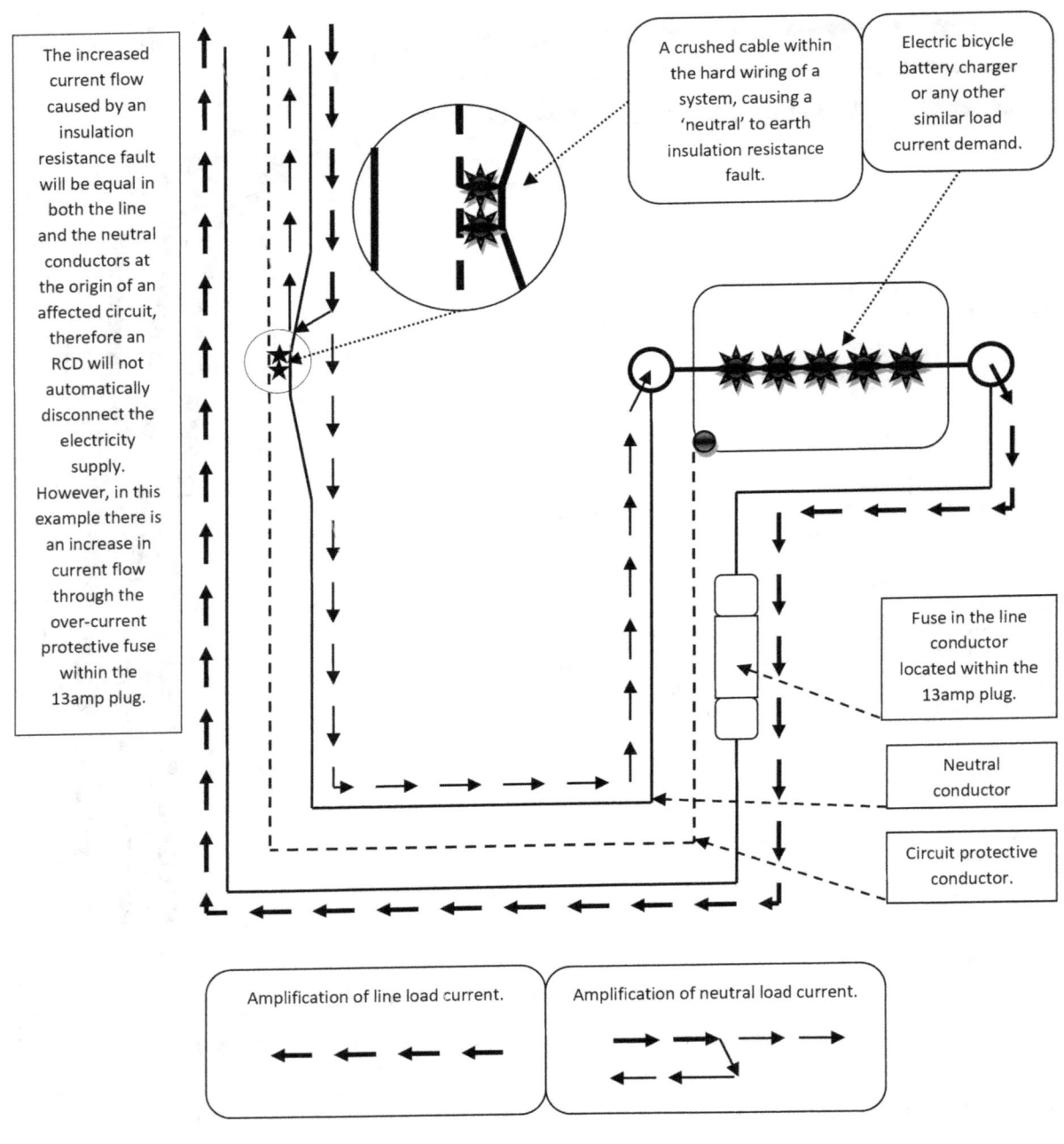

The increased current flow caused by an insulation resistance fault will be equal in both the line and the neutral conductors at the origin of an affected circuit, therefore an RCD will not automatically disconnect the electricity supply. However, in this example there is an increase in current flow through the over-current protective fuse within the 13amp plug.

A crushed cable within the hard wiring of a system, causing a 'neutral' to earth insulation resistance fault.

Electric bicycle battery charger or any other similar load current demand.

Fuse in the line conductor located within the 13amp plug.

Neutral conductor

Circuit protective conductor.

Amplification of line load current.

Amplification of neutral load current.

Remembering that; conventionally we speak of current flow as moving from line to neutral, but the motion at an atomic level is from neutral to line. A 'neutral' to earth insulation resistance fault will cause an increase in load current demand through the 'line' conductor within an appliance supplied by the affected circuit, therefore the over-current protective 'fuse' located within the 13amp plug will rupture and automatically disconnect the electricity supply to the appliance before any damage occurs.

*The 'current imbalance' at the origin of an affected circuit will 'not' be of a great enough magnitude to cause the RCD to automatically disconnect the supply.

Insulation Resistance Faults and Their Relationship with an Increased Load Current Demand #2

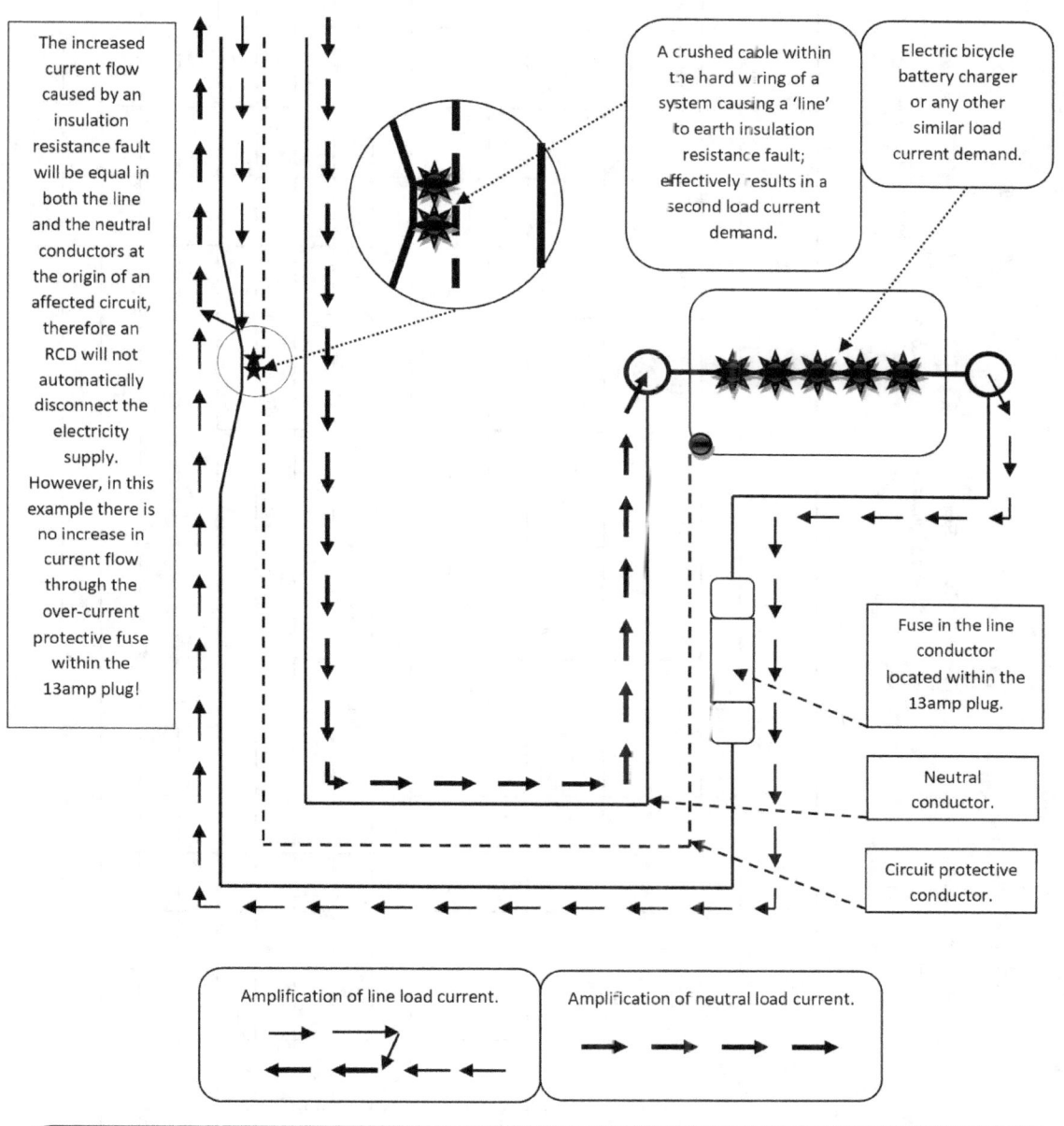

The increased current flow caused by an insulation resistance fault will be equal in both the line and the neutral conductors at the origin of an affected circuit, therefore an RCD will not automatically disconnect the electricity supply. However, in this example there is no increase in current flow through the over-current protective fuse within the 13amp plug!

A crushed cable within the hard wiring of a system causing a 'line' to earth insulation resistance fault; effectively results in a second load current demand.

Electric bicycle battery charger or any other similar load current demand.

Fuse in the line conductor located within the 13amp plug.

Neutral conductor.

Circuit protective conductor.

Amplification of line load current.

Amplification of neutral load current.

Conventionally we speak of current flow as moving from line to neutral, but the motion at an atomic level is from neutral to line. Therefore; a second load current demand caused by an insulation resistance fault between 'line' and earth will increase the load current through a 'neutral' conductor which has no over-current protective fuse within the 13amp plug! As a result; in this set of circumstances the over-current protection of the entire affected circuit becomes crucial as the MCB (or fuse) within the distribution board is relied upon to automatically disconnect the electricity supply and so protect the circuits' cabling from being exposed to a 'small overload of a long duration'!

*The 'current imbalance' at the origin of an affected circuit will 'not' be of a great enough magnitude to cause the RCD to automatically disconnect the supply.

FORM WR5

Form No xxxx/5

INSTALLATION SCHEDULE (including Test Results)

Contractor......*T.S.Mann*..........

Test Date......*XX/XX/XXXX*..........
Signature.....*XX..XXXX*..........

Address of Installation
XX.XXX.XXXXXXX..........
XXXXXXXXX.XXXXXX..........
XXXX..XXX..........

Instruments:
r.c.d. tester..........
continuity..........
insulation..........
others.......... *XXXXXXXXXXXXX*

1 Type of Supply TN-S TN-C-S TT
2 Ze at origin...*0.19*..........ohms
3 PSCC......*1.25*..........kA

Items to be disconnected before testing..........

Electrical Installation Safety & Efficiency Test

Description of work completed / Circuit	No of points	Overcurrent Device type	Rating A	Breaking capacity kA	Cable Size mm²	CPC mm²	Lgth m	Continuity Ω R1 + R2	R2	Insulation Resistance MΩ Phase/Neutral	Phase/Earth	Neutral/Earth	Earth Loop Imp. ZT Ω	RCD IΔn mA	mS	Polarity	Remarks
4	5	6	7	8	9	10	11	12	13	14	15	16	17	18	19	20	21
1 *SHOWER*	1	B	40	6	10	4	7	0.10	0.04	>299	>299	>299	0.31	30	32.7	√	R.C.D. - #A
2 *S.S.O. (K)*	12	B	25	6	2.5	1.5	15	0.13	0.08	>299	>299	>299	0.35	30	28.9	√	R.C.D. - #A
3 *LIGHTS (D)*	6	B	6	6	1.0	1.0	20	1.74	0.22	>299	>299	>299	1.01	30	28.9	√	R.C.D. - #A
4																	
5 *COOKER*	1	B	25	6	6.0	2.5	6	0.12	0.08	>299	>299	>299	0.36	30	20.1	√	R.C.D. - #B
6 *S.S.O.*	27	B	25	6	2.5	1.5	35	0.45	0.30	>299	>299	>299	0.69	30	20.8	√	R.C.D. - #B
7 *LIGHTS (U)*	8	B	6	6	1.0	1.0	28	1.85	0.24	>299	>299	>299	1.08	30	20.7	√	R.C.D. - #B
8																	
9																	
10																	
11																	
12																	

22 Main bonding check: Gas..√ ... Water..√ ... Other..... √ .... size..*10*.....mm²

23 Main Earth size..*16*......mm²

24 Earth Electrical Resistance...*0.18*.......Ω

Deviations from Wiring Regulations and special notes:

Page 5 of 5 pages

Evaluation of the Example Test Results

On the previous page is an example of a genuine Installation Schedule. There are in fact five pages that need to be completed in total, but the information required to fill in the first four pages can all be recorded at the office and will not change over time, whereas the information on this 'fifth' page needs to be verified repeatedly as an electrical installation will deteriorate with the passing of time. Understanding your test results will allow you to 'maintain' any electrical installation up until there is a requirement to re-wire that system:

Type of supply TN-S/TN-C-S/TT #1, PSCC (kA) #3, Circuit #4, Number of points #5, Overcurrent Device; Type #6, Rating (A) #7, Breaking capacity (kA) #8:

In this example; '#1 type of supply (TN-C-S)' system; the '#8 breaking capacity (6.0kA)' of the MCB's (miniature circuit breakers), was confirmed as being greater than the '#3 perspective short-circuit current (1.25kA)' as required to be fit for purpose. The chosen overcurrent protective MCB's are of an appropriate '#6 type (B)' and '#7 rating (40/25/6)' to effectively protect the '#4 circuits' and '#5 the number of points' on each, from "small overloads of a long duration" as required by Regulation.

Ze at origin (ohms) #2, Main bonding check (mm²) #22, Main Earth size (mm²) #23, Earth electrical resistance (Ω) #24:

The external earth resistance '#2 Ze at origin (0.19Ω)' was confirmed as being of a greater value than the '#24 earth electrical resistance (0.18Ω)'. The main earthing conductor (16.0mm²), the main earth bonding conductor (10.0mm²) and the supplementary bonding conductor (4.0mm²) cross-sectional areas were all confirmed as being appropriately sized. There were no interruptions in continuity between any extraneous-conductive-parts of this example installation and its' main earthing point. Therefore; if a line conductor should for any reason contact an extraneous-conductive-part it will cause a fault of negligible impedance to earth and so in this example installation, the supply will be automatically disconnected within the maximum Regulation standard disconnection time of <0.4 of a second as required by Regulation.

Cable size; line and neutral conductors (mm²) #9, circuit protective conductor (mm²) #10, length (m) #11, Continuity; (R1 + R2Ω) #12, (R2Ω) #13, Earth loop impedance (ZT Ω) #17:

Circuit #1; is a shower circuit supplied by 10.0mm²/4.0mm² cable which has line and neutral conductor continuity values equal at 0.06Ω and a circuit protective conductor value of 0.04Ω, resulting in an R1 +R2Ω resistance value of 0.10Ω at a length of around seven metres, with a ZT Ω earth loop impedance value of 0.31Ω.

Circuit #5; is a cooker circuit supplied by 6.0mm²/2.5mm² cable which has line and neutral conductor continuity values equal at 0.04Ω and a circuit protective conductor value of 0.08Ω, resulting in an R1 + R2Ω resistance value of 0.12Ω at a circuit length of around six metres, with a ZT Ω earth loop impedance value of 0.36Ω.

Circuit #2; is a switched socket outlet circuit in the kitchen supplied by a 2.5mm²/1.5mm² ring final circuit, with cabling that has line and neutral conductor continuity values equal at 0.05Ω and a circuit protective conductor value of 0.08Ω, resulting in an R1 + R2Ω resistance value of 0.13Ω at a circuit length of an estimated fifteen metres, with a ZT Ω earth loop impedance value of 0.35Ω.

Circuit #6; is a switched socket outlet circuit providing general-purpose power to the rest of the house supplied by a 2.5mm²/1.5mm² ring final circuit which has line and neutral conductor continuity values equal at 0.15Ω and a circuit protective conductor value of 0.30Ω, resulting in an R1+ R2Ω resistance value of 0.45Ω at a circuit length of an estimated thirty-five metres, with a ZT Ω earth loop impedance value of 0.69Ω.

Circuit #3; is the downstairs lighting circuit supplied by 1.0mm²/1.0mm² cabling having un-switched line, neutral, and circuit protective conductor continuity values equal at 0.22Ω and a switched line conductor value of 1.52Ω, resulting in an R1 + R2Ω resistance value of 1.74Ω at a circuit length of an estimated twenty metres, with a ZT Ω earth loop impedance value of 1.01Ω.

Circuit #7; is the upstairs lighting circuit supplied by 1.0mm²/1.0mm² cabling having un-switched line, neutral, and circuit protective conductor continuity values equal at 0.24Ω and a switched line conductor value of 1.61Ω, resulting in an R1 + R2Ω resistance value of 1.85Ω at a circuit length of an estimated twenty-eight metres, with a ZT Ω earth loop impedance value of 1.08Ω.

Comparing the recorded R1Ω and the R2Ω values of Circuit #1:

Recorded as being 0.06Ω and 0.04Ω we can see that the <u>smaller</u> 4.0mm² circuit protective conductor has a <u>lower</u> resistance at 0.04Ω than the larger 10.0mm² line and neutral conductors at 0.06Ω, with all three conductors being of the same approximate length??? Well; I did warn you that this job can get quite interesting at times. As always, recording the 'highest' available values take precedence and in this example those values include the resistance offered by the double pole shower isolating switch, which effectively increases the line and neutral measured continuity values and just gives the impression that the conductors of the greater cross-sectional area also have the greater resistance!

Comparing the recorded R1 + R2Ω and R2Ω values of Circuits #2 & #6:

We can confirm that Circuit #6 is most certainly the longer of the two ring final circuits having higher recorded continuity values of 0.15Ω and 0.30Ω compared to 0.05Ω and 0.08Ω for Circuit #2, and that the conductors of the greater cross-sectional area have consistently the lower resistance values.

Comparing the recorded R1 + R2Ω and R2Ω values of Circuits #3 & #7:

We can confirm that Circuit #7, the upstairs lighting is the longer circuit of the two having the higher recorded continuity values of 1.85Ω and 0.24Ω compared to 1.74Ω and 0.22Ω for Circuit #3. There is a two-way switch controlling the final light fitting on each of these two circuits and the inclusion of the resistance of the associated 'strapping' cables has significantly increase the measured R1Ω and therefore the calculated R1 + R2Ω values to 1.74Ω and 1.85Ω, respectively.

Comparing the recorded R1Ω and the R2Ω values of Circuit #5 with those of Circuits #2 & #6:

We can see a consistent ratio between the recorded continuity values of 0.04Ω for the 6.0mm² line and neutral conductors and 0.08Ω for the 2.5mm² circuit protective conductor of Circuit #5, that (virtually) 'mirror' the ratio between the 2.5mm² line and neutral conductors and 1.5mm² circuit protective conductors of Circuits #2 and #6, which have recorded line and neutral conductor values of 0.05Ω and 0.15Ω and circuit protective conductor values of 0.08Ω and 0.30Ω respectively.

Insulation resistance; Phase/Neutral #14, Phase/Earth #15, Neutral/Earth #16 (M Ω):

Although measured values are allowed by Regulation standards to be as low as 0.5M Ω for, for example; an electrical installation in an old wooden barn with no other incoming services, owned by a farmer who only uses that installation once in a year where the cost of remedial work may be prohibitive. If any measured values should drop below >200M Ω in a 'normal' electrical installation, the affected system will be so wasteful that you should consider the cabling to be 'damaged' and therefore, replaced for the sake of your clients' electricity bill as well as for the sake of the planet!

In this example installation; insulation resistance testing was conducted on every circuit from the distribution board.

A damaged cable was found and replaced during this example test, then the test was recommenced with all the circuits' measured values being recorded as; >299M Ω.

Earth loop impedance (ZT Ω) #17, Continuity tests; (R1 + R2Ω) #12, (R2Ω) #13:

Comparing the measured earth loop impedance values (ZT Ω) recorded in column #17 with the continuity (R1 + R2Ω) and (R2Ω) values recorded in columns #12 & #13:

In a healthy power circuit; the measured earth loop impedance value (ZT Ω) increases and decreases circuit by circuit at a similar rate and in a similar ratio to the calculated continuity value of R1 + R2Ω and the measured continuity value of R2Ω, with the ZT Ω being consistently a greater value than the calculated R1 + R2Ω value.

In a healthy lighting circuit; the extra resistance of the 'switch' in the 'switched line' conductor (R1Ω) can increase the calculated continuity value of R1 + R2Ω to a figure that is 'greater' than the 'total' measured earth loop impedance value (ZT Ω), even though the earth loop impedance test is carried out through far the longer conductors (than the continuity test) and includes the 'external' earthing conductor/electrode resistances (Ze Ω)!

The most important difference between 'continuity' testing and 'earth loop impedance' testing is the temperature of the cabling whilst each of these tests is carried out; the cabling remaining at 'room' temperature whilst continuity testing is undertaken with the power 'off,' as opposed to the cabling being at 'operating' temperature when earth loop impedance is tested with the power 'on.'

With the circuit switched 'on' whilst earth loop impedance testing:

At 'operating' temperature; any loose connections or warn out switches and socket outlets will wastefully produce 'heat' causing electrical conductors to expand to fill any gaps and therefore, effectively 'maintain' the measured impedance value (ZT Ω) of a circuit!

With the circuit switched 'off' whilst continuity testing:

At 'room' temperature; any loose connections or warn out switches and socket outlets will cause noticeably high measured (and therefore also calculated) continuity resistance values (R1Ω, R2Ω and therefore also R1 + R2Ω), when compared to other electrical conductors of a similar length and cross-sectional area either within the same circuit or in other similar circuits.

Evaluating the recorded example 'earth loop impedance (ZT Ω) #17' test results and; comparing example 'earth loop impedance (ZT Ω) #17' test results with example continuity (R1 + R2Ω) #12 and (R2Ω) #13 test results:

Circuit #1 (shower) and Circuit #5 (cooker) have ZT Ω values of 0.31Ω and 0.36Ω therefore; although these two circuits are of a similar length (7 and 6m) the larger cross-sectional area 10.0mm²/4.0mm² shower supply cable has the lower ZT Ω value (as you would hope), even though; the double pole shower isolating switch significantly increased the measured R1Ω and therefore the calculated R1 + R2Ω resistance values during the earlier 'continuity' test!

Circuit #2 (kitchen sockets) and Circuit #6 (general-purpose sockets) have ZT Ω values of 0.35Ω and 0.69Ω therefore; this confirms that the general-purpose socket outlet circuit #6 (that snakes around the whole house) is much the longer circuit having by far the greater ZT Ω value, as well as by far the greater recorded R1 + R2Ω value of 0.45Ω compared to 0.13Ω for circuit #2 during the 'continuity' test.

Circuit #3 (downstairs lighting) and Circuit #7 (upstairs lighting) have ZT Ω values of 1.01Ω and 1.08Ω therefore; the upstairs lighting is confirmed as being the longer of the two circuits having the greater ZT Ω value and, when these values are compared to the much greater recorded R1 + R2Ω continuity values of 1.74Ω and 1.85Ω for these two circuits, you can see by just how much even 'brand new' (though inexpensive) two-way switches can adversely affect measured continuity resistance values (R1Ω); when the power is switched 'off' and the conductors are only at 'room' temperature.

None of the earth loop impedance test measurements (ZT Ω) on this example Installation Schedule exceed their Regulation standard tabulated maximum values, which will always be the case when the correct type of cable has been chosen for any application! Regulation standard maximum tabulated earth loop impedance values are based on maximum voltage drop and maximum voltage drop is the overriding factor when calculating maximum circuit 'lengths.' Therefore; the Regulation standard maximum 4% 'Volt Drop' has not been exceeded in this example, this systems' current usage has therefore been minimised, and; the maximum automatic supply disconnection times will satisfy the Regulation standard of <0.4 of a second during a fault of negligible impedance to earth.

Residual Current Device (RCD) #18 (mA) #19 (mS):

In this example installation, residual current device (RCD) testing was conducted from each point of every circuit. As you can see from this example Installation Schedule; disconnection times (recorded at the 'rated' tripping current) from identical residual current devices, can vary (approximately 30mS for RCD #A and approximately 20mS for RCD #B) even when tested in identical circumstances.

Polarity #20:

'#17 Earth loop impedance (ZT Ω)' tests, and '#19 RCD (mS)' tests; from every point of each circuit of this example installation, also confirmed that there were no problems with crossed Polarity.

*In this example installation therefore; Regulation standard fundamental requirements for safety have been satisfied and so; the primary goal of providing reasonably practicable electrical efficiency has/will be 'safely' achieved.

Fire Alarm System Economy; (Systems Remaining Functional in a

Tall Building for '>One Hour' after Catching Fire)

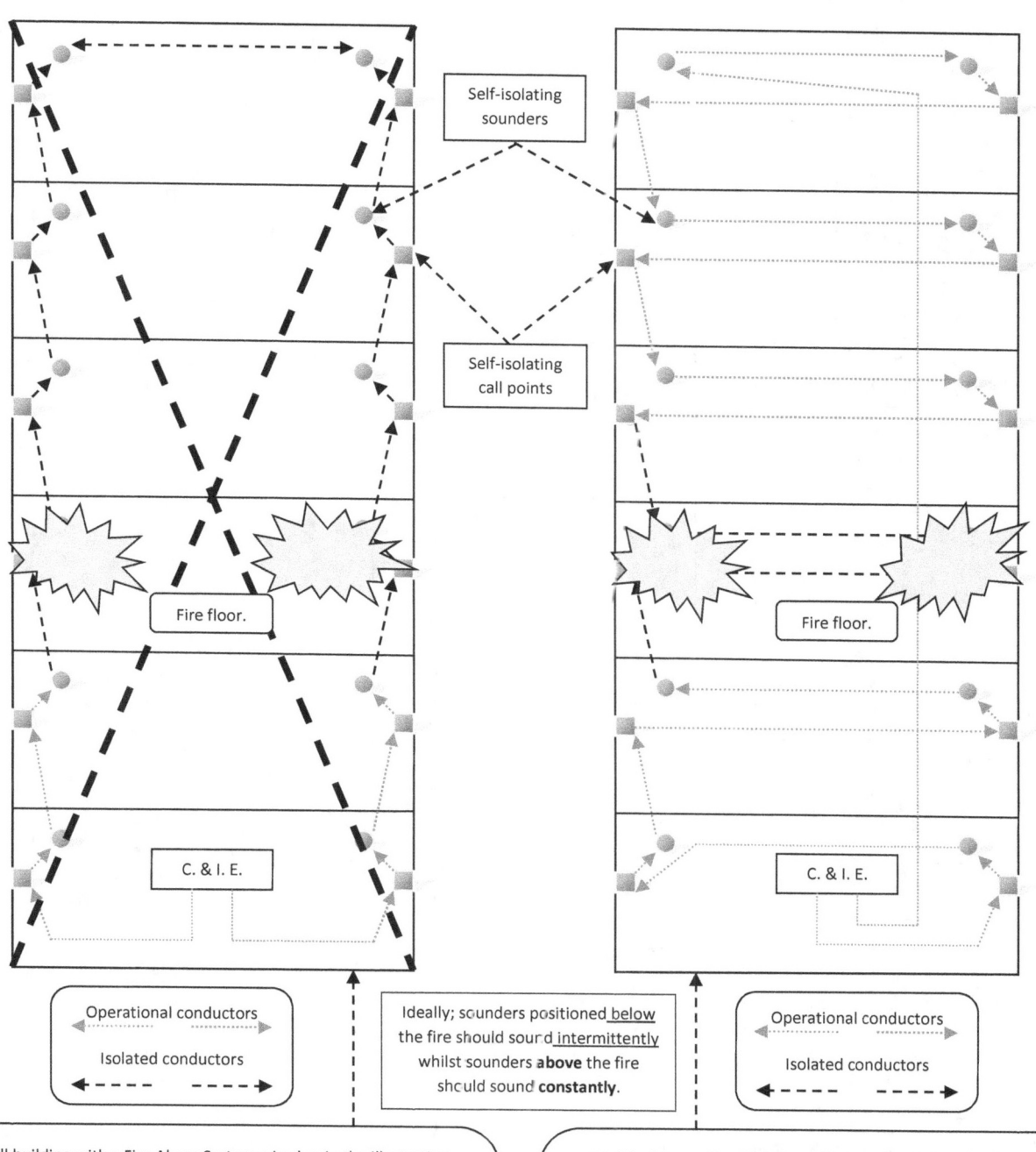

Self-isolating sounders

Self-isolating call points

Fire floor.

Fire floor.

C. & I. E.

C. & I. E.

Operational conductors

Isolated conductors

Ideally; sounders positioned _below_ the fire should sound _intermittently_ whilst sounders **above** the fire should sound **constantly**.

Operational conductors

Isolated conductors

A tall building with a Fire Alarm System wired as in the illustration above, will be _vulnerable_ to a fire on one floor cutting the system in half and leaving the area above the fire in complete silence, and; with all its' self-isolating call points permanently rendered inoperable. The addition of non-self-isolating automatic detectors will make no difference, as super-heated smoke can destroy all the component parts of the system on one floor faster than any automatic detectors above the fire can activate the Control and Indicating Equipment.

A tall building with a Fire Alarm System wired as in the illustration above, will be _invulnerable_ to a fire on one floor cutting the system in half, and; all the self-isolating components that are not actually on fire will remain operational for at least 'one hour' after the system itself catches fire. The addition of non-self-isolating automatic detectors will have a positive impact in this example because the smoke from the fire will eventually trigger the first 'still functional' automatic detector it comes to on any floor above the fire floor.

On-board Vehicle Battery-Bank Charging; (Wind Turbines, Rotating Wheel/Stationary Axle Generators, KERS & Solar Panels)

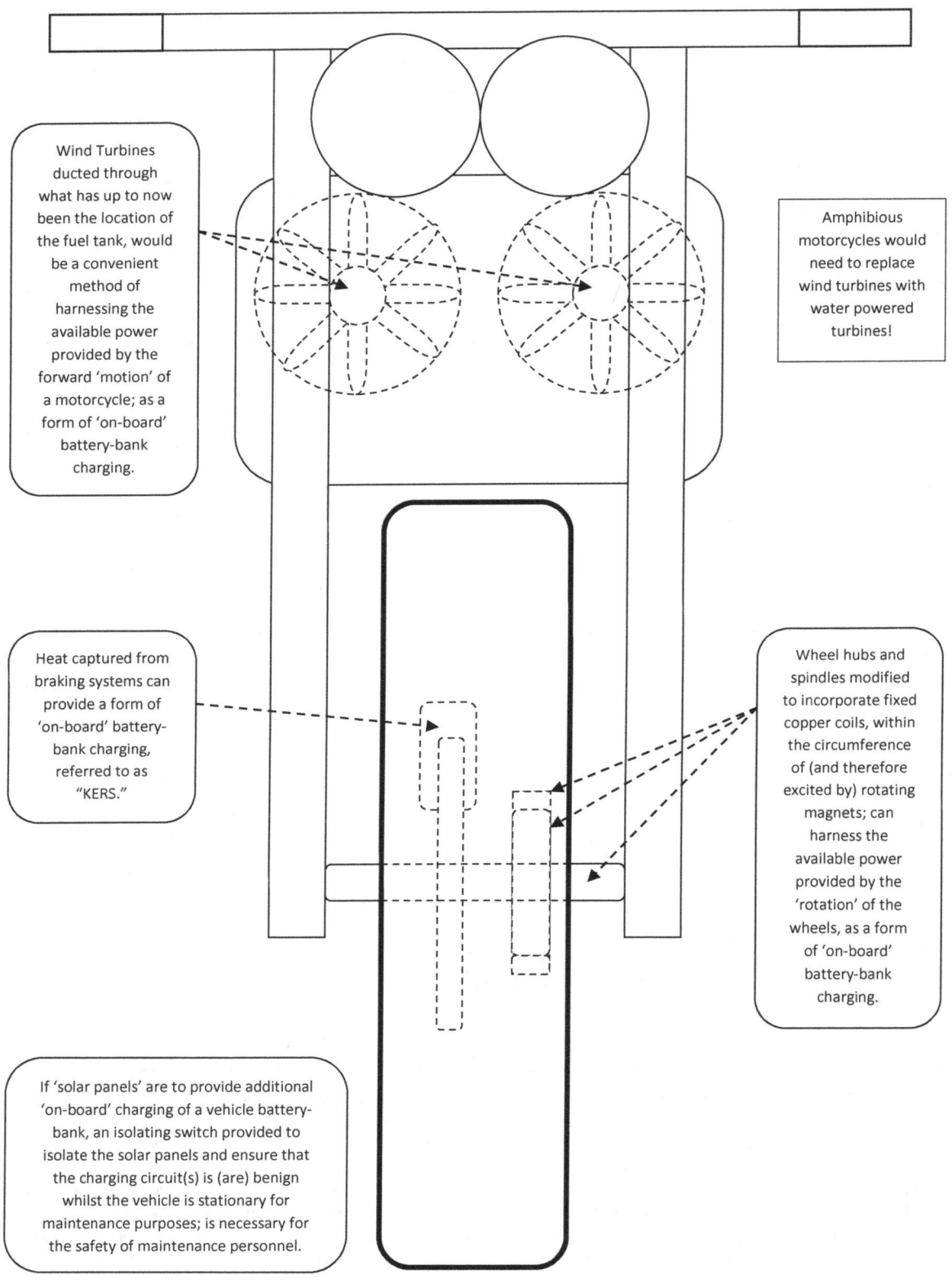

Wind Turbines ducted through what has up to now been the location of the fuel tank, would be a convenient method of harnessing the available power provided by the forward 'motion' of a motorcycle; as a form of 'on-board' battery-bank charging.

Amphibious motorcycles would need to replace wind turbines with water powered turbines!

Heat captured from braking systems can provide a form of 'on-board' battery-bank charging, referred to as "KERS."

Wheel hubs and spindles modified to incorporate fixed copper coils, within the circumference of (and therefore excited by) rotating magnets; can harness the available power provided by the 'rotation' of the wheels, as a form of 'on-board' battery-bank charging.

If 'solar panels' are to provide additional 'on-board' charging of a vehicle battery-bank, an isolating switch provided to isolate the solar panels and ensure that the charging circuit(s) is (are) benign whilst the vehicle is stationary for maintenance purposes; is necessary for the safety of maintenance personnel.

Multiple DC Electric-motor Powered Crankshaft

Below is a simplified representation of any 1/2/3/4/5/6/8/10/12-cylinder internal combustion engine, with the crankshaft powered by pistons.

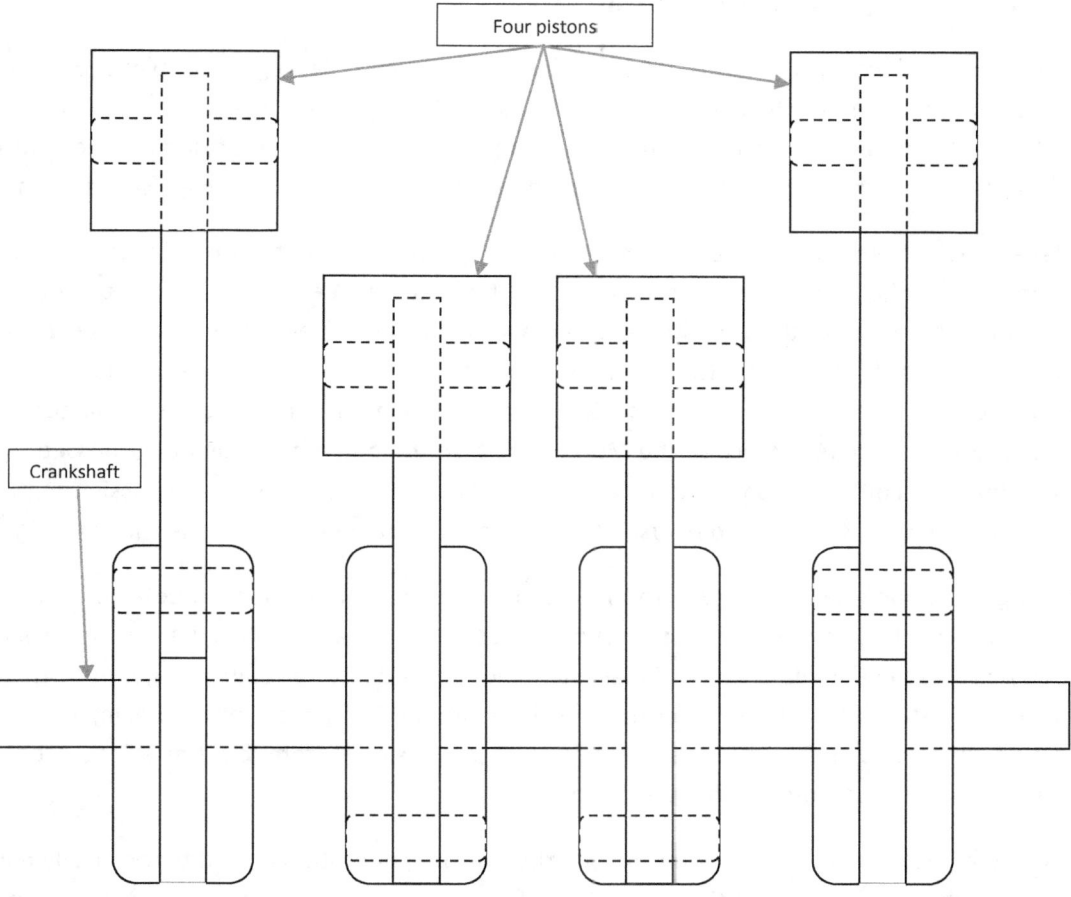

Below is a simplified representation of any 1/2/3/4/5/6/8/10/12-DC Electric-motor powered crankshaft, with each DC electric-motor producing the same amount of power as the pistons driving the crankshaft above.

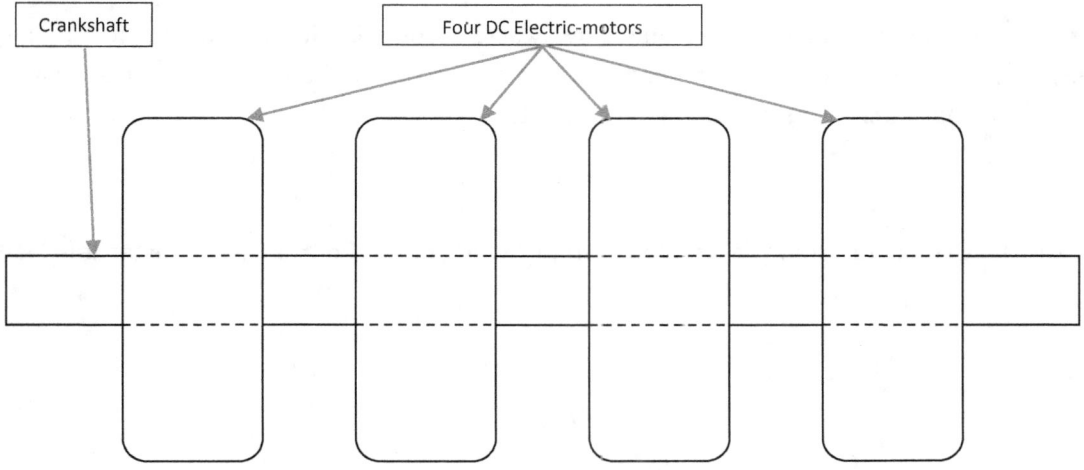

Conclusion

Looking at the bigger picture; with regards to the supply, distribution, and use of 'green' electricity it becomes clear that our success now, would theoretically allow the future of Humankind to 'outlive' the stored atomic energy within our own Sun!

Humankind can produce Hydrogen from wind turbines within the Polar regions of planet Earth and store it at a temperature of -240°C, which is the best part of 200°C colder than the current ambient temperature in those regions. Consequently, it is therefore feasible for humankind to take control of the ambient temperatures of the Earths' ice caps and so 'stabilize' or even 'reduce' sea levels at will.

Once planet Earths' general-purpose electricity supply is powered almost entirely by harnessing the gravitational pull of the Moon (with a little help from the light/heat generated by the Sun close to the equator and the force of the wind in the icy areas), all our fossil fuels, biofuels, and nuclear power can be used as fuel for propulsion systems designed for use in the aerospace industry. The gravitational pull of the Moon influences the liquid water of planet Earth only because planet Earth is located 'inside' the circumference of the Moons' orbit, so the power that can be harnessed from the gravitational pull of the Moon can only be harnessed on planet Earth; whereas fossil fuels, biofuels, and nuclear power can also be used 'outside' of the circumference of the Moons' orbit.

The next region of our Solar System where there appears to be an abundance of potential fuel sources would have to be around the planet Jupiter, so I would hazard a guess that the aerospace industry is going to need a fair amount of fossil fuel, biofuel, and nuclear power to get us to this next available 'gassing station!' A nuclear-powered turbine combined with fossil or biofuel injected into a compression chamber can provide a fair range for a jet propulsion system; but the Solar System is a massive place, and Jupiter must be halfway across it!

If Humankind can get as far as the planet Jupiter; then future generations could theoretically have access to enough alternative potential types of fuel for us to have reached another Solar System by the time our Sun finally runs out of atomic energy and implodes!

Therefore:

If it risks leaving Humankind short of getting halfway across our Solar System; wasting fossil fuels, biofuels, and/or nuclear power now, is "a crime against the future of humanity" because it means Humankind will be 'stuck' around this one tiny planet!

The death of a Star is only 'a wonderous thing' when observed from a safe distance☺

INSTALLATION SCHEDULE (including Test Results)

Contractor..................

Test Date.................... Address of Installation

Signature....................

....

Items to be disconnected before testing..................

| 1 Type of Supply TN-S TN-C-S TT |
| 2 Ze at origin..................ohms |
| 3 PSCC..................kA |

| Instruments: |
| r.c.d. tester.................. |
| continuity.................. |
| insulation.................. |
| others.................. |

Description of work completed	Circuit	Overcurrent Device			Cable			Test Results												
		No of points	type	Rating A	Breaking capacity kA	Size mm²	CPC mm²	Lgth m	Continuity Ω		Insulation Resistance M Ω				Earth Loop Imp.	RCD			Polarity	Remarks
									R₁ + R₂	R₂	Phase/Neutral	Phase/Earth	Neutral/Earth		ZT Ω	IΔn mA	mS			
	Circuit	5	6	7	8	9	10	11	12	13	14	15	16		17	18	19	20	21	
	4																			
	1																			
	2																			
	3																			
	4																			
	5																			
	6																			
	7																			
	8																			
	9																			
	10																			
	11																			
	12																			

22 Main bonding check: Gas...... Water...... Other...... size........mm²

23 Main Earth size........mm²

24 Earth Electrical Resistance..................Ω

Deviations from Wiring Regulations and special notes: